SHORE FISHING

Shore Fishing

A GUIDE TO CARDIGAN BAY

by

John Mason

WITH DETAILED FISH ID GUIDE

Coch-y-Bonddu Books
2013

SHORE FISHING
A Guide To Cardigan Bay

by John Mason

© First published by Coch-y-Bonddu Books, 2013

Cover painting © David Miller

ISBN 978 1 904784 54 8

Published and distributed by
Coch-y-Bonddu Books Ltd, Machynlleth, Powys SY20 8DG
01654 702837
www.anglebooks.com

CONTENTS

FOREWORD   7

ACKNOWLEDGEMENTS   8

FIRST CAST   9

INTRODUCTION   11
   Cardigan Bay and responsible sea angling

A PRACTICAL GUIDE TO FISHING IN CARDIGAN BAY   15
   An overview of shore fishing in the region

Tackle: rods, reels, lines, hooks, sinkers
and all the rest – and a little on cameras   17

Sourcing bait   43

Wind, weather and tides: the forces that shape
the marine environment in Cardigan Bay   51

The fishing grounds: how to fish them   63

   How Cardigan Bay was formed   63
   Shallow sandy beaches   68
   Steep shingle beaches   74
   Mixed ground   78
   Shallow reefs   82
   Deep water rock marks   85
   Estuaries   92
   Man-made structures   98

A TOUR AROUND CARDIGAN BAY   103
  A guide to the best fishing locations

  The basic layout of the bay: south to north   105
  South-west Section: Ramsey Sound to Cardigan   107
  South central Section: Cardigan to Aberystwyth   118
  North central Section: Aberystwyth to Barmouth   128
  North-west Section: Barmouth to Bardsey Sound   134

THE FISH SPECIES OF CARDIGAN BAY   147
  How to catch and identify them

  Bass   150
  Breams   157
  Cod family   158
  Silver and conger eels   166
  Flatfish   169
  Minor predators   175
  Triggerfish and wrasse   183
  Mini-species   186
  Mullet   186
  Rays   188
  Sharks   192
  An historical note   198

Photographic guide and essential information   200

LAST CAST   271

Books on sea angling have tended to concentrate on tackle, rigs and techniques that can be applied universally to the many and varied species of sea fish that swim in the waters that surround the British Isles.

Few of them make any reference to the effects of geography and geology, the topography of the sea bed and the adjacent coast, tidal ranges and currents, and all the other local features that have such a great influence on the behaviour of both resident and migratory species of fish.

In my extensive travels around the coasts of Britain, fishing many and varied venues, I have been struck by how different regions have their own idiosyncrasies, and by how valuable is the 'local knowledge'; the hard-earned experience of lifelong resident anglers like John Mason, in translating the published generalities into regular success, both for themselves and for their fellow anglers; locals and visitors alike.

In *Shore Fishing: A Guide To Cardigan Bay*, John Mason shares his in-depth knowledge of tactics and locations and, by pointing the reader in the right direction right from the start, gives him the benefit of his many years of experience. John expresses all this in a lively and entertaining manner in an enjoyable book that will certainly result in greater successes for sea anglers visiting Cardigan Bay.

Derek Townsend
2012

Derek Townsend is the author of *Bass Fishing from the Shore in South East Wales*

ACKNOWLEDGEMENTS

My heartfelt thanks go to Derek Townsend for contributing the Foreword; Duncan Bamford, Rod Calbrade, Gareth Davies, Kevin Doughty, Chris and Adam Doyle, Dr Jim Ellis, Steve Hambidge, Karen Hancox, Dave Hellewell, Paul Morgan, Gethyn Owen, Gareth Pickard, Ian Pratt, Tim Rapley and Carl and Pam Worrall for supplying images of fish that I didn't catch in the two years since this project was conceived; and Paul Morgan and Paul Curtis of Coch-y-Bonddu Books for taking the project on. And of course, all of the many fishing buddies with whom I have bagged-up, shivered away dark biteless nights with or spent time conversing with in person or online. You know who you are!

Thanks also to fish and wildlife artist, David Miller, for supplying a copy of his painting, *Feeding Frenzy*, a detail of which appears on the front cover of this book. www.davidmillerart.co.uk

In addition, this work was supported by Wild Fishing Wales, www.wildfishingwales.com. Sign up online to receive a quarterly email from Wild Fishing Wales bringing you all the latest news on sea, game and coarse fishing in Wales.

It's getting late. I wind in my line and unhook two undersized whiting. Scrambling down barnacled rocks to the edge of the sea I slip the fish back in, perhaps to put on more weight, to be eaten by seals or gannets or to have the life crushed from them in the claws of some industrial fishing vessel. The low sun casts a path of burning gold across the water from Cardigan Island to my feet. It's warm for the time of year. A splash out there and I look up to see dolphins, working as a team to herd mackerel as they have done for countless millennia. They come within thirty metres of our rocky perch. One is obviously working for the Welsh Tourist Board. It accelerates upward through the green water to become airborne in the middle of Sunset Strip. It's clear of the sea and I see golden droplets cascade from its silhouetted dark flanks as it hangs there suspended on my memory. Night falls and we head for home and humanity. Out there, the slow beat of tides and seasons goes on. The rhythms of the Earth: great unseen wheels, turning slowly and surely, always there, beyond our control. On our return – from one world back to another – we find that Man U have lost and that beer's gone up. Some of the lads are visibly distressed …

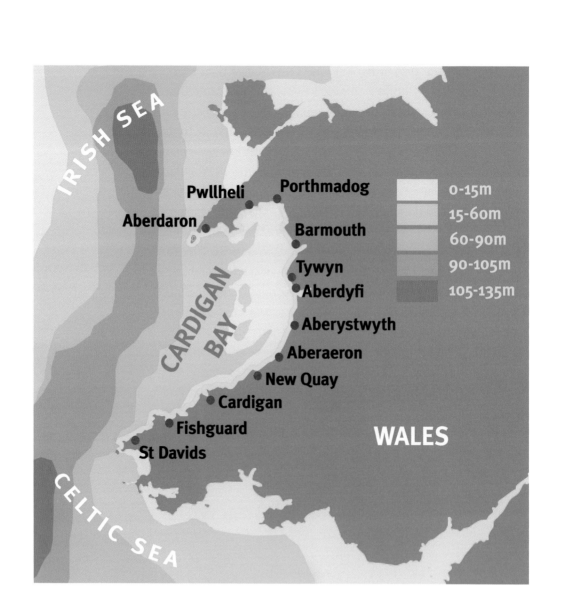

IRISH SEA

Pwllheli

Porthmadog

Aberdaron

Barmouth

CARDIGAN BAY

Tywyn

Aberdyfi

Aberystwyth

Aberaeron

New Quay

Cardigan

Fishguard

St Davids

CELTIC SEA

WALES

	0-15m
	15-60m
	60-90m
	90-105m
	105-135m

_____ **INTRODUCTION** _____

Cardigan Bay is the broad, concave sweep of coast that connects Ramsey Sound in the south-west to Bardsey Sound in the north-west corners of Wales respectively. The distance between the two points (via the All Wales Coast Path) is over 200 miles – giving a tremendous range of potential fishing venues. There are miles of shallow, clean, sandy surf beaches, interrupted in places by tracts of mixed ground where the sand is densely strewn with weed-covered boulders. There are extensive shallow reefs of deeply gullied rock that uncover and dry with each low tide. Locally, there are steep shingle beaches offering access to deeper water, with the greatest depths of all being found off the craggy headlands that occur at various points around the bay. Finally, there are the estuaries, where the rivers of the west coast, large and small, meet the sea.

Such a variety of fishing venues (known as 'marks') means in turn a great variety in the species of fish available to both the resident and visiting angler – the author caught 40 different species from the Welsh shore in 2009 and reckons that with a level of dedication verging on obsessive, fifty could be a realistic twelve-month target from the Cardigan Bay coast. But most of the time we fish for relaxation, exercise and the chance to catch supper.

This guide does not tell you to fish Mark X from two hours before high tide to three hours after. It concentrates instead on each of the different ground-types, explaining the best approach to each and what you are likely to catch there, and also how they respond to changes in seasons and conditions. The methods detailed are all based on first hand experience over the years. It catalogues the fish most likely to be found in the Bay and effective methods with which to catch them, with photographs of over sixty species to help identify what you catch. How venues are actually fishing at any given time (and the seasons do vary a lot from year to year as weather patterns fluctuate) is best answered by asking around, either online or at local tackle shops. Here, we focus firmly upon understanding the marine environment, weather and tides, approach and methods. Understand these things and, if the fish are there, you should have the odds on your side.

Responsible sea angling

Sea angling with baited hooks has been a human activity since prehistoric times and today it is one of the UK's biggest participation sports. I use the term 'sport' loosely here – for me it has always been about hunting for my supper. Properly done, line catching of edible fish is the most selective fishing method of all. Baits and tackle can be selected with the appropriate species and size in mind and thus 'discards' are kept to a minimum and are returned alive, with a high chance of survival. Discards from mechanised industrial fishing methods run into many thousands of tonnes of dead 'by-catch' per year in UK waters alone – a situation that the word 'ridiculous' utterly fails to address. What an appalling abuse of such a fine natural resource. Line-catching makes sense in all sorts of ways. Indeed, it's about taking direct personal responsibility for the fish that you eat – or if a commercial fisher who concentrates on line-catching (and increasing numbers are), the fish that you sell.

Shore angling does not currently require any licence and the only rules as such (outside of local bylaws in a few spots) are with regard to salmon, sea-trout, protected species such as eels and the two shads (uncommon, herring-like fish) and the minimum legal sizes of the various fish species. That degree of freedom is valuable, but with freedom there always comes responsibility. The responsibilities in shore angling are simple. Firstly; do not cause unnecessary suffering to fish – kill those intended for eating swiftly upon landing. The fact that most fish (apart from those caught by man) end their days by being eaten alive by other predators with various degrees of mangling in the process does not alter that obligation. Secondly; keep only what you can realistically use, either by eating straight away or by storage (e.g. freezing). Do not waste this valuable natural resource. Thirdly; you are a guest of the marine environment and in many cases, on somebody else's land. If you were invited round to dinner at a friend's house, would you depart from there having left behind heaps of half-eaten food, beer cans, plastic bags and worse all over their floor? Would you leave behind lengths of line with baited hooks that their cat or dog would find and swallow with the obvious consequences? Of course not, so apply the same standards to the coast. It is pleasing to note that some angling suppliers are taking steps to tackle the litter problem: the frozen bait supplier Ammo has initiated a scheme where for every twenty empty bait-packets returned to a participating tackle-shop a free pack of Ammo bait is provided in exchange. This is a good incentive: however, the bottom line is that you can always tell when a good angler has been at a venue – he or she has left no sign that they had been there. That should be all that needs to be said on the matter.

And finally; keep safe. My thirty years of shore angling experience has taught me some useful lessons in that department that I will be sharing later in these pages.

A practical guide
to fishing in Cardigan Bay

Scissors, knives
Long-nosed pliers
Artery forceps
T-bar disgorger
Tape measure, scales
Fish clonker, cloth

Hooks, sharpening stones, beads

Main lines

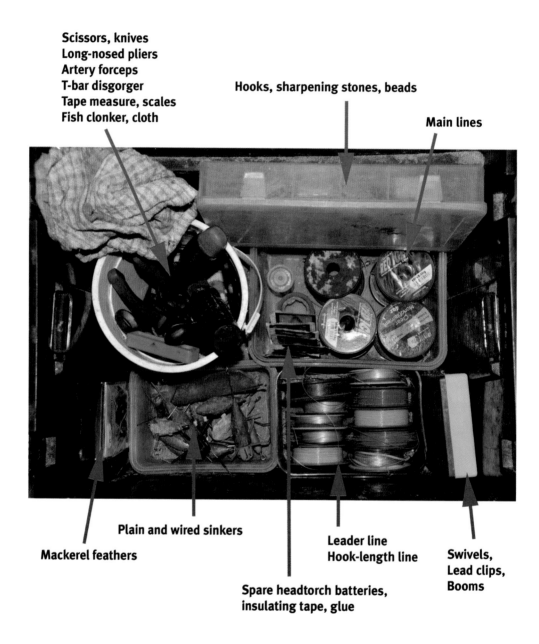

Plain and wired sinkers

Mackerel feathers

Leader line
Hook-length line

Swivels,
Lead clips,
Booms

Spare headtorch batteries,
insulating tape, glue

TACKLE

This section is essentially aimed at those who are thinking of taking up shore angling and thus consists of general, non-specialised advice. If you give fishing a go and find that you like it, you will tend, through time, to develop your own preferred style. I know people who almost exclusively flyfish for bass, for instance, but would not recommend that as a starting point to someone who has never handled a rod before. Instead, let's see how a beginner should be kitted out for the Cardigan Bay shore.

Rods and Reels

As a bare minimum you will of course need a rod and reel. There are dozens of brands and scores of models to choose from with costs between a few tens into the hundreds of pounds. Don't let this put you off. A perfectly functional 12ft beach rod and reel can be bought as a combination for less than fifty pounds at many tackle shops and in addition there are often some great second-hand bargains to be found. The fish have no idea how much the rod cost or whether it is currently fashionable!

A beach rod (or beachcaster) is designed primarily to hurl a lead sinker, typically 4oz to 6oz in weight, an acceptable distance out to sea, and do so without breaking. In many cases a distance of 40 to 80 yards is quite adequate as the fish are closer in than a lot of people realise – the interface between land and sea being a focus for biodiversity and therefore food. Now, the UK casting record is something over 300 yards. But that's not on a beach with a rainy force 5 south-westerly in your face – it's on a measured casting court, for casting has become a popular quasi-athletic field event in its own right. To reach such phenomenal distances requires technically superior equipment plus the same combination of strength, speed and coordination that is needed by an Olympic athlete sending a javelin, discus or hammer soaring off into the sky. If such activities interest you, there are casting clubs dotted around the country where you can develop the necessary skills. For a beginner on the beach, a good plan is to team up with somebody who has already fished a bit and hopefully they will show you the ropes – or better still, search online and find your nearest casting instructor. Just a session or two of instruction will help you develop a good, safe style right from the start. Rarely is money better spent. As time goes by your technique and distance will improve, and since any beachcasting rod is capable of hitting a hundred yards plus, you will soon have that extra range capability if needed.

Rod length is a matter of choice but for general shore-fishing, think of 12ft as a happy minimum. There are a lot of longer rods, up to 16ft or more, on the market these days, but they tend to be more expensive: personally I like using them for a whole number of reasons but in almost all instances I would nevertheless have caught the same fish with a twelve footer. A lot of anglers use a pair of rods – the idea behind this being that by having different baits out at different distances a wider range of potential species can be fished for. This is fine on a flat sandy beach – however if you are fishing from a precipitous rock ledge over deep water and double figure conger eels simultaneously snaffle the baits on both rods, you will have a big problem on your hands. Matching tactics to the circumstances is the trick.

Reels for beachcasting come in two varieties – the multiplier and the fixed spool. These both have the job of delivering line smoothly when casting and retrieving it efficiently whilst reeling in, with or without a fish on the end of the line – but they do it in different ways. The multiplier has a revolving, bearing-supported spool onto which the line is wound via a hand crank and gears. The rotation of the spool is controlled by braking and drag systems and by disengaging the gear drive – putting the reel into 'free spool'. Casting with such a reel requires a certain amount of practice. When uncontrolled, the spool can end up turning faster than the sinker is pulling away line. This inevitably results in loose coils of line forming on the spool, one of which will then catch on something, bringing everything to a crashing halt, with the sinker's forward motion often snapping the line in what is referred to as a crack-off. Such an event transforms the spool into a spectacular mess of loops and loose ends of line which is known to all and sundry as a 'bird's nest'. Not fun.

Multipliers are most useful over deep, rough ground where the target is big fish – they are strong reels and have very easily adjustable drags so that a lunging fish can take line under pressure. Over such ground, casting distance is often less important in any case, but the fast retrieval speed of a modern multiplier is useful for getting your tackle up through the water, clear of the myriad snags below.

For the beginner who just wants to try fishing on a beach, a fixed-spool reel is a much better bet. At one time, these were regarded as highly inferior to multipliers but technology and materials have come on apace and well-engineered yet relatively affordable fixed-spool reels are now supplied by most tackle manufacturers. As its name suggests, the spool does not rotate – instead, line is wound onto it by a rotating bail-arm which is disengaged clear of the spool when casting. Get your tackle dealer to demonstrate this in the flesh. Most models have a drag system for controlling bigger fish. Although they are not as bombproof as multipliers, they will easily handle most of the regular species that you will encounter on our beaches. The good thing for beginners is that they are easy to cast with and tangles are rare – just be sure not to overload them with line. A good rule of thumb is to leave a gap of an eighth of an inch between the end of the line and the lip of the spool.

Line

Monofilament line is cheap and reliable as long as it is not abused. This means checking it regularly for signs of abrasion which can be caused by floating debris, moving shingle, barnacled rock and so on. If your line feels rough to the touch then replace it – if you don't it may break unexpectedly and that could mean losing a good fish. You can buy 'mono' in all sorts of breaking strains from very light up to 250lb test or more. Don't let this confuse you. Over clean sand, 15lb breaking strain will do nicely; for mixed areas with sand, stones and weed 20-30lb is fine and for ultra-rough ground where big fish are expected, many anglers use 40-50lb line 'straight through', meaning not having a stronger leader tied onto the end of the main line.

A leader is a length of stronger line (usually around 40ft long), that has one main purpose – to take the shock-loading of a powerful cast. Try hurling a 6oz sinker out on 15lb main line and lots can go wrong. For starters the line is thin enough to cut your fingers, but worse it could break during any point of the cast, sending the sinker flying off in any old direction. On a crowded pier or beach the potential results of heavy lead weights flying around randomly at high speed are not worth contemplating. Your leader should be chosen by the simple formula of 10lb breaking strain for each ounce of lead. Thus, a 5oz sinker requires a 50lb leader – and so on. Leaders can be bought in bulk spools or as sets of specially tapered lengths – the latter better for smooth casting but more expensive, so a bad idea over snaggy ground. They often come in bright or 'dayglo' colours, which can be useful on a dark winter's night when that extra bit of visibility helps. Tie the leader to the main line with a blood knot – there's plenty of instructions online for that, or get the tackle shop to show you how. Wind it on until there are eight to ten turns of leader on the reel's spool and you are ready to think about the next step – sinkers, hooks and so on – terminal tackle, or the stuff on the business-end of the line.

Sinkers, swivels, beads, hook-lengths and hooks

Sinkers are streamlined lead weights with an attachment loop of thick wire sticking out of the top. They serve two purposes of equal importance – to provide the weight for casting, and to hold the terminal tackle down on the seabed afterwards. Cheapest are plain lead sinkers, which are fine if you don't mind the bait moving about a bit (sometimes, on clean ground, that can be useful). If you want to nail the bait in one place on the seabed though, because of snags or strong tides, there are two types of grip-leads available. One has fixed wires – the other is the so-called 'breakout-lead', in which the wires will spring free under a certain amount of pressure from the rod tip. The latter is used most commonly since in most cases in Cardigan Bay the tides are not so severe as to need anything more serious. Weight-wise, carry a range from 3oz to 6oz and you will have most situations covered. If conditions are such that a 6oz sinker will not hold then it's likely to be too rough to be worth fishing in any case.

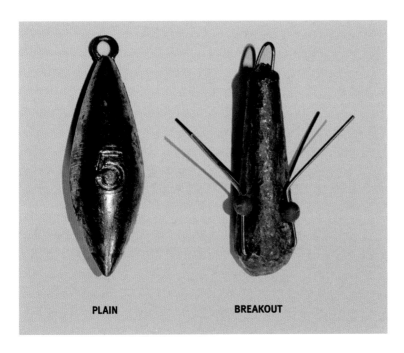

PLAIN   BREAKOUT

Plain and breakout sinkers

Swivels are useful little gizmos for connecting the various parts of your end tackle together. They consist of either two or three metal rings (to which line may be tied) connected to a central pivoting joint. Two-way swivels connect your leader to a length of line of the same breaking strain (your 'rig body') which has to take the power of the cast too. Off the rig body comes the attachment points for the sinker and the hook-lengths. For sinkers, many anglers use snap-link swivels, which are swivels with locking clips attached to one end, although there are tailor-made lead-clips available too. For attaching hook-lengths, three-way swivels can be used, or alternatively two-way swivels held captive on the rig body by metal crimps and plastic beads threaded onto the line and clamped tight at the desired point. Just be sure to get swivels of the right size: a swivel of thinner gauge wire than the line you intend to tie to it will act as a cutting edge, so make sure swivel wire is thicker than line at all times. Some anglers like to use plastic or metal booms, similarly held captive on the rig body, to the ends of which the hook-lengths are tied.

Hook-lengths are best made from clear monofilament and there are several brands available in a range of breaking-strains, the selection of which depends on what you're fishing for. Most of the fish you will encounter from Cardigan Bay's beaches will be easily landed on 25lb mono, so it's worth having a spool of that. Toothier species like bull huss can chew through such line but will struggle to do so if you double up. Very toothy species like conger eels require a no-nonsense approach and hook-lengths of 100lb mono or stronger (looks a bit like strimmer cable), or even wire are the norm. Use tucked half blood knots (again look for online tutorials, or get the tackle dealer to show you) to attach hook-lengths to swivels and hooks alike. I've never had a single one fail. Very heavy mono and steel traces supplied by tackle dealers are typically crimped to the swivels and hooks, although some brands of heavy mono can still be knotted – it depends on their stiffness.

Both sinkers and lines may be advertised for sale in imperial

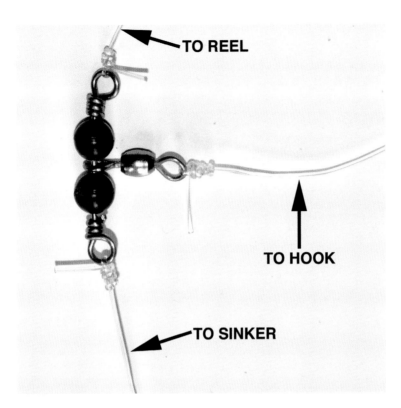

TO REEL

TO HOOK

TO SINKER

Left:
A three-way swivel
This is one way of attaching a hook-length to the rig body

Below:
Crimped two-way swivel
Another way of attaching a hook-length to the rig body

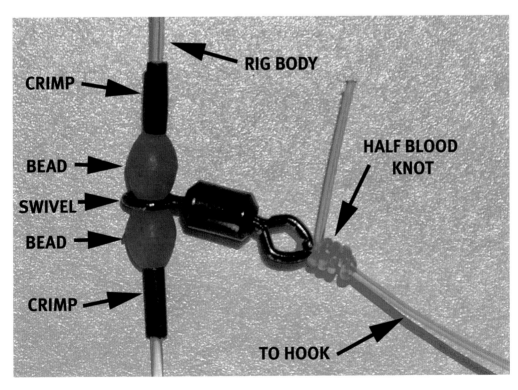

RIG BODY

CRIMP

BEAD

SWIVEL

BEAD

CRIMP

HALF BLOOD KNOT

TO HOOK

or metric terms and monofilament is sometimes referred to by its diameter. The following table gives conversions for some commonly used values and gives typical thicknesses for lines, although these do vary slightly from brand to brand.

Monofilament lines			Sinkers	
lbs	kg	mm	oz	g
5	2.27	0.2	2	56
15	6.82	0.4	3	85
25	11.36	0.5	4	112
50	22.73	0.7	5	140
100	45.45	1.0	6	170

Hooks come in a range of patterns and sizes. They need to be chosen bearing in mind the type of fish targeted (and consequently the type and size of bait used). Hook sizes sometimes confuse beginners because the scale used to rank them runs in both directions. Small hooks start at size 1 and run on, getting smaller and smaller, into the 20s – the latter mostly used in specialist coarse fishing. All you will need for most sea angling situations are a variety from size 1 down to size 6. Larger hooks start at size 1/0 (a bit bigger than a 1) and run up to 14/0 or more – giant 'meat hooks' like the latter being for big game fishing, large sharks and so on. On the shore, 6/0 is generally as big as you will need to go. Have a selection up to that size and you'll be sorted.

Hook patterns vary from the small, fine wire 'Aberdeen' hooks (ideal for flatfish, whiting and other non-thuggish stuff), to medium-sized fairly fine but strong hooks such as the 'Viking' pattern (ideal for fish like bass and rays), up to the strong, forged hooks of heavy-gauge wire, such as the 'O'Shaughnessy' and 'Limerick' patterns, required for more feisty/heavy species like conger eels. Again, carry a range. Hooks are available in plain or, in some cases, stainless steel. In the undesirable event of

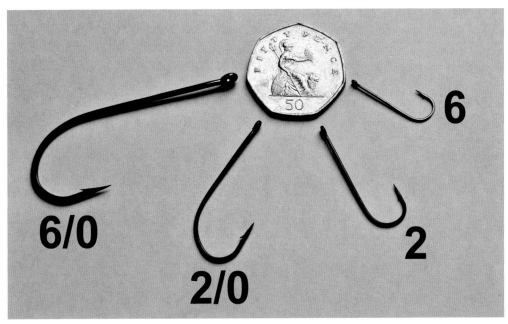

6/0

2/0

6

2

a fish getting away with a hook in it, plain steel will rust away quite quickly as sea water is pretty corrosive stuff, whereas stainless will not. Stick to plain. Above all, make sure your hooks are sharp (whetstones are cheap) and put rusty ones to one side as they can snap if badly corroded.

Hook sizes
Shown in the range typically used for shore angling with a 50p for scale

Introduction to shore-fishing rigs

Rigs come in all shapes and sizes and can be bought ready tied or made up at home. Most shore-fishing rigs are variations of two basic types – leger and paternoster.

With a leger rig, the sinker is attached above the hook-length, whilst with a paternoster the opposite is the case – the lead is at the end. Leger rigs tend to be single hook affairs, the aim being to nail the bait hard on the seabed, to catch fish that feed exclusively on the bottom, like flatfish and rays. The lead can either be fixed thus – end of leader followed by two-way swivel followed by short length of rig body (with plastic bead, snap-link swivel and a second plastic bead all sliding on it) then a second two-way swivel and your hook-length. Or, the snap-link

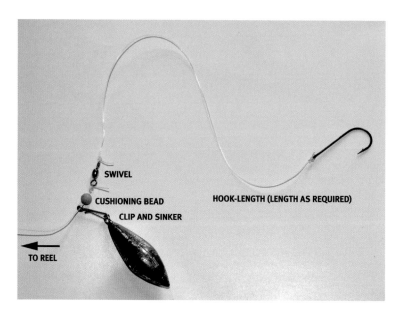

SWIVEL

CUSHIONING BEAD

HOOK-LENGTH (LENGTH AS REQUIRED)

CLIP AND SINKER

TO REEL

A running leger rig

and one bead are slid onto the end of the leader and then the two-way swivel to the hook-length is tied on – this is a running leger that allows a fish to take line without coming up against the dead weight of the sinker, which could in theory spook it into dropping the bait. The plastic beads protect knots against moving metal items such as swivels, which could cause the knots to weaken by repeated pounding otherwise. They are dirt cheap, so be sure to have plenty. I keep mine in an old 35mm film canister.

Paternoster rigs have one or more hook-lengths spaced apart above the sinker at appropriate distances so that they don't tangle together during the cast. In very shallow water at any great distance from the rod tip, the baits will all be on the bottom. In deeper water, especially close-in, the baits further up the rig will fish higher in the water. This can be quite important for some species – indeed, some anglers go a step further by adding a stopped floating bead near the hook of the top hook-length, making that bait bob well up off the bottom. Floating bead rigs can be very effective for predators like garfish and fish that feed along the upper parts of weed beds, like black

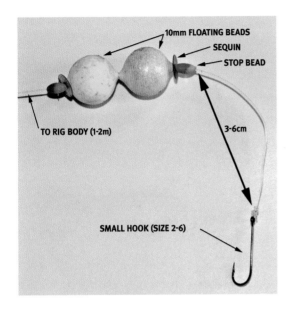

10mm FLOATING BEADS

SEQUIN

STOP BEAD

TO RIG BODY (1-2m)

3-6cm

SMALL HOOK (SIZE 2-6)

Left:

Floating Beads

A hook-length equipped with floating beads, in order to get the bait fishing high up in the water - where mackerel and garfish will take it

Below:

A simple Paternoster rig

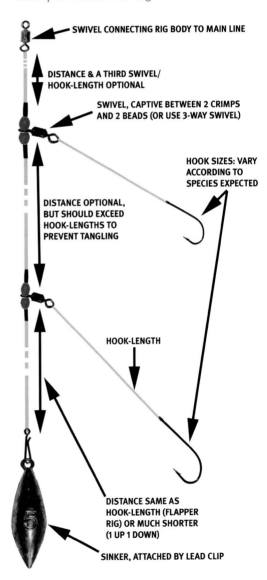

SWIVEL CONNECTING RIG BODY TO MAIN LINE

DISTANCE & A THIRD SWIVEL/ HOOK-LENGTH OPTIONAL

SWIVEL, CAPTIVE BETWEEN 2 CRIMPS AND 2 BEADS (OR USE 3-WAY SWIVEL)

HOOK SIZES: VARY ACCORDING TO SPECIES EXPECTED

DISTANCE OPTIONAL, BUT SHOULD EXCEED HOOK-LENGTHS TO PREVENT TANGLING

HOOK-LENGTH

DISTANCE SAME AS HOOK-LENGTH (FLAPPER RIG) OR MUCH SHORTER (1 UP 1 DOWN)

SINKER, ATTACHED BY LEAD CLIP

bream. If you are fishing deep water and do not want baits to fish up in the water, pay out a little slack so that although the line is not taut you will still detect bites – or use a leger rig.

The number of hook-lengths you use in your rig is up to you. What you are fishing for and what baits you want to use are the main factors in deciding how many but, in general, three or less are manageable whilst more than that are rarely used. How long a hook-length you use will determine the behaviour of the bait on the seabed. Short hook-lengths of 6 inches or less will keep a bait static whilst if you want your bait to wave enticingly about, use longer ones of up to 2ft. For small baits, single hooks are best whilst for large baits, such as a whole squid, two hooks in tandem are often preferable. The latter is known as a Pennell rig. It stops the bait sliding down to form a messy blob that obscures the hook point. It also hooks fish that attack long baits from the 'wrong' end and would otherwise be missed. Slide on the top hook then tie on the bottom one. The distance between the two can vary but typically it is one to three inches. The top hook is held in place by sliding some tight plastic rig tubing over the line and the hook shank, or tightly winding on a few turns of telephone wire.

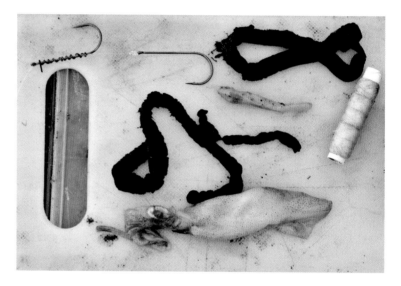

Before and after: **Big bait tactics** *a large bait combining black lugworm, squid and razorfish presented on a twin-hook Pennell rig incorporating 5/0 hooks. Bait elastic is essential to stop the bait disintegrating in mid-cast and also to present a streamlined offering with plenty of hook point protruding.*

Paternoster or leger hook-lengths may be deployed as they are – they will flap about during the cast – or 'clipped down'. The latter term means that the rig includes bait clips, which hold the baited hooks by their bends and are either built into swivels and sinkers or incorporated as stand-alone items. A typical stand-alone bait clip is fixed onto the rig body with tight rubber tubing, so that it can only be slid up or down by heavy applied thumb-and-finger pressure. This means that when correctly adjusted the hook-length will be quite tight to it during the cast, but when the rig hits the water, the impact and deceleration will shake the hook free. Specialist rigs, such as the so-called 'long and low', employ cunning arrangements of bait clips: the 'long and low' involves two bait clips facing in opposite directions.

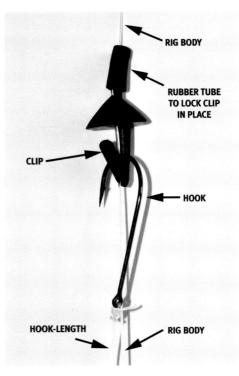

A bait clip

A long hook-length is tied to a swivel near the bottom of the rig, the hook-length then goes up over one bait clip at the top of the rig and down again past the swivel, where the hook is tensioned onto a second, downward facing bait clip. With such a rig, ultra-long (6ft plus) hook-lengths may be cast out without the tangling that would normally occur. However, the chief advantage of any clipped down rig is that it is streamlined, the greatly reduced drag when it is airborne meaning that it can be cast a lot further. This streamlining also reduces the risk of the bait disintegrating during the cast. However, the best way to prevent bait disintegration is to lash it securely to the hook with fine elastic thread. A spool of bait elastic, available in any good tackle shop, will cost no more than a pound or two, so make sure you have one in your tackle box. Without it, some soft baits like crab or shellfish are virtually impossible to use.

Float fishing can be fun and most tackle shops stock a good

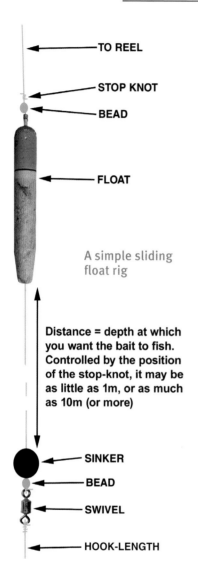

TO REEL

STOP KNOT

BEAD

FLOAT

A simple sliding
float rig

**Distance = depth at which
you want the bait to fish.
Controlled by the position
of the stop-knot, it may be
as little as 1m, or as much
as 10m (or more)**

SINKER

BEAD

SWIVEL

HOOK-LENGTH

range of floats. Alternatively, you can fashion your own from a lump of polystyrene. Floats can be fixed to the line with rubber bands although most bought varieties have a hollow tube running up the inside through which the line goes. A sliding float like this has to be stopped at some point otherwise the bait will sink all the way to the bottom, defeating the object of the exercise. Stopping a float is accomplished by a plastic bead on the line above the float, stopped by a bit of knotted mono above it on the main line, knotted rubber band or special small 'stop bead'. These can all be slid up or down the main line under thumb-and-finger pressure but should not move on their own. As they dictate where the float stops on the main line, they also dictate the depth at which you are fishing – an important factor. A few small weights – drilled bullet sinkers of 1/4oz or 1/2oz depending on the size of the float – will carry the bait down to the feeding-zone and ensure that the float sits properly upright in the water. Slide them onto your main line after the float, add a plastic bead to cushion the knot, then tie on a swivel and attach your hook-length to it, and you're ready to go.

Essential bits and pieces

Although many anglers prefer to hold their rods for bite detection, a tripod rod rest is in any case useful for keeping everything off the sand whilst changing rigs or re-baiting. A tape measure is important for checking your catch meets the size regulations and is therefore legal to take home (the current size limits for individual fish species are provided in the identification guide).

Scales will be required if you want to know the exact weight of your catch. For killing fish for eating, a sharp, heavy clonk on the head with a length of heavy steel pipe or wood does the job instantly – do not leave fish to gasp their way out of life over many minutes. A sharp knife for gutting the catch, scissors for cutting line or bait and artery forceps, stout long-nosed pliers and strong T-bar hook disgorger for unhooking the fish completes the kit. Many anglers stash all this stuff into a seat box which neatly doubles as carrying container and something to sit on, but where more arduous approaches are required to reach marks a rucksack is far better and, when climbing down steep rocks, much safer.

Because many species are more likely to be caught at night a few extra items are required. Decorate your rod tip with reflective tape – it'll be easier to see. Get a good head torch – there are plenty of LED models available today – and always carry some spare batteries in a sealed poly-bag. Finally, warm clothing is a must for those long winter nights, unless you want to be in a state varying between miserable and hypothermic. Humans lose an awful lot of body heat especially from their heads, so a good warm hat is a must, and fingerless gloves will keep your hands warm whilst allowing you to sort out bait, tie knots and so on. In terms of footwear, wellies are useful for many situations but chest waders are better on shallow beaches. For rock fishing, where grip is paramount, stout boots with good soles and ankle support are essential. A brightly-coloured waterproof floatation jacket will give you a chance should you be unfortunate enough to fall in. At remote rocky locations, mobile reception is often non-existent and a pack of distress flares may be your only means of raising the alarm in the event of something going badly wrong.

Food and drink should not be neglected. On a hot summer's day, venues that require a stiff climb can easily see you become dehydrated. Take plenty of water – not beer – to replace fluid loss. Alcohol and fishing are not a good mix: apart from the safety factor a few beers will lead to carelessness.

Enjoy a couple of pints after a session, not during it! For cold winter nights a flask of hot soup will help make life bearable. Conversely, blazing sunshine by the sea can easily cause bad sunburn so have a tube of sunblock stashed away in readiness.

Artificial bait fishing

The previous paragraphs dealt mainly with tackle for fishing with bait. There is however another option – artificial bait fishing, in other words using lures that mimic prey items so convincingly that predatory fish are conned into attacking them. Lure fishing can work all year round but is best done in the warmer months of the year, at first light and at dusk, when predators are most active and the baitfish most abundant. Smaller rods and reels are used – a 9ft to 10ft rod and small fixed spool reel typically, and lighter line of 10lbs or less unless really big fish are expected.

Lures fall into a number of categories. Hard lures include spinners, spoons, bars, wedges and pirks. These are usually made of steel that has been painted or anodised in various metallic colours. The weight and shape of each individual lure affects its casting distance and determines its action in the water. Soft lures are usually made from various plastic and rubber compounds and they require extra weight to be added for casting unless you are working very close in. They include all sorts of imitation fish, from sandeels to shads, in every colour combination under the sun. Adding weight for casting distance is done by fishing the lure in a paternoster or leger-style rig, the weight of the sinker determined by the range at which you intend to fish. Special hooks allow some soft lures to be rigged 'weedless' – the hook point lying flush against the lure body, where it is much less likely to snag on anything. This is very useful when deep spinning over and through beds of kelp and other kinds of seaweed.

Plugs are typically made of plastic or wood and are designed to fish at different depths from the surface to deep, this being

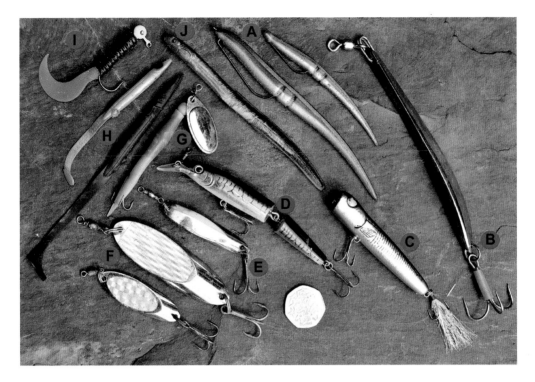

A selection of lures from the author's 'most-used' box.
Clockwise from top: A) soft Slug-go lures rigged Texposer-style to avoid weed; B) a chromed casting-pirk for deep, fast water; C) a surface-popper plug; D) a jointed plug; E) a slimline wedge; F) standard Dexter Wedges; G) 'Flying Condom' spinner; H) Red Gill and Eddystone eels – the original soft lures; I) a Jellyworm with weighted head and J) a Sidewinder shimmer sandeel

determined by the buoyancy of the plug body and the shape of the metal or plastic 'lip'. They are also designed to wobble as they are retrieved through the water, like a wounded fish. Although relatively expensive, they are effective catchers and plugging can be addictive, to the extent that some people switch to it to the exclusion of everything else.

Lures do not only work by appearance, something that is amply demonstrated by the fact that they work at night, too. Predatory fish often hunt effectively in poor visibility because they have the ability to home in on a source of vibration. Well-designed lures, both soft and hard, capitalise on this by giving off vibrations that con predators into thinking that a baitfish is swimming by, triggering them into attack mode.

When choosing lures, it's best to get an up-to-date idea of how your target area is fishing and what lures in what colours

Bagging-up
When the mackerel are inshore, sets of feathers are the quickest way to catch them in numbers

are scoring. It does vary. At different times of year, the fish feed on different varieties of prey – and it makes sense to use lures that imitate that prey. During the summer and autumn months in Cardigan Bay, anything that credibly impersonates a sandeel will catch bass or pollack. Or you can try to imitate slightly larger prey species by using a wedge, whose long-casting properties are also useful when you can see the predators swirling on the surface 50 yards out. So a selection of plastic eels and wedges is not a bad start. They are reasonably-priced, too.

Whether followers of natural or artificial bait techniques, anglers should carry a few sets of mackerel feathers. These are hooks dressed with feathers or tinsel, tied into strings of four or more with a swivel at one end and a clip for the lead at the other. It's very important when buying feathers to check the breaking strain of the rig body. Some feather rigs are designed for boat fishing and are built from only 20lb breaking strain line. Shore fishermen need 50-60lb to avoid any disasters due to line breakage during casting. From late spring through into autumn, shoals of mackerel can suddenly show up at any time and having feathers to hand gives you the option to quickly switch tactics and target them if desired.

Tactics for artificial bait fishing

The art of careful observation is probably the most important talent that successful lure fishers develop and use to their advantage. Of obvious importance is the need to determine whether the predators are feeding at surface or deeper down. Surface feeding is self-evident with swirls, splashes and predators and prey jumping out of the water. If the fish are expected to be there, but no surface activity is visible, they may be feeding in mid-water or close to the sea bed. So the key is to fish at the appropriate depth. To keep a lure close to the surface, start retrieving the moment it hits the water. To ascertain depth, wait for the lure to splash down and then, with it freely able to take line, count how many seconds it takes to sink to the sea bed. Then you can countdown on subsequent casts in order to determine the depth at which you begin the retrieve. If it took twenty seconds to reach the seabed, a countdown of ten seconds before the retrieve starts will see the lure fishing in a mid-water position – and so on.

In very deep areas, where tidal rips are fished at medium to long range, it pays to begin by searching the entire water column, fanning out casts to cover as much of the area as possible until you locate the fish. Once you know where they are, keep the casts going to the same area and at the same depth. Where the predators are charging about on the surface, don't cast right into the middle of them – they will get spooked, dive in unison and maybe go off the feed. Instead, cast over them into the water beyond and slightly ahead of them and then bring the lure back so that it passes just in front of them. In areas of fast tides, let the lure run in the same direction as the tide is running – baitfish mostly tend to swim with the tide and not against it and a lure doing something unnatural will tend to make predators suspicious.

Retrieval speed will affect the actions of different lures in different ways. As a general point, if you want to fish a lure deep, retrieve it very slowly. Conversely, a fast retrieve starting immediately upon splashdown has a lure splashing and hopping across the surface – which is very effective for some species. The later chapter about the various fish species includes tips with respect to the most effective lure fishing techniques. An additional technique involves fishing a lure by the 'sink-and-draw' method, where the lure is pulled upwards and forwards by an upward sweep of the rod, then is allowed to flutter downwards as the rod-tip is lowered and line is retrieved. This works well with wedges, as the erratic movement resembles that of a wounded baitfish, which will often trigger an attack.

Saltwater flyfishing

Flyfishing, for bass, mackerel, pollack, garfish and even mullet has become an increasingly popular activity over recent years, yet it is one branch of sea angling in which I have little experience. However, my publisher, Paul Morgan, is an experienced flyfishing enthusiast. I'll happily let him share that enthusiasm with you. In fact, having read the following, I might well take it up myself! Over to Paul:

"Stand, knee-deep, in the shallow water of a small river-mouth on a summer evening with the fins and tails of fish breaking all around. Most of these are mullet, waiting for the tide to carry them farther up the estuary, but some are bass, searching for crabs among the stones and harrying the shoals of sand-eels and smelts that gather in such places. Occasionally a silver fish leaps clear of the water: it may be a restless mullet but is more likely to be a sewin, eager to taste the fresh water of its birth. Our target here is the bass; most will be schoolies to be carefully returned to the water, but there is always the possibility of a five-pounder that will explode in the shallows and empty your reel as it flees for deeper water and safety.

This is shallow water, close range fishing, and the flyrod is the ideal tool to present the small weightless baitfish imitations that work so well. If you are a flyfisher you will already have

the minimal equipment needed to take advantage of this most exciting of Cardigan Bay's angling adventures. Any flyrod designed for reservoir trouting will do the job – a seven- or eight-weight coupled with a weight-forward eight floating line is ideal. One could go lighter but the heavier outfit helps to cast larger flies and will cut through an onshore breeze. Don't bring your favourite Sage – or your Hardy Brothers reel, though. More than once I have had to use my rod butt as a wading staff as I made my way back to dry land after some rather too adventurous wading. There are modern plastic or graphite flyreels on the market for just a few pounds that will do admirably. In fact your whole outfit needn't cost more than fifty or sixty pounds.

Flies can be simple, too. For bass many of us stick to two or three favourite patterns; white lures about two inches long that represent the small whitebait and sandeels that are the favourite prey of bass. Many patterns have been developed for saltwater fishing overseas: bonefish in the tropics, striped

Fly-caught bass
Some anglers become addicted to this way of fishing

Happy hunting
ground
*Estuary mouths can
provide excellent
sport for flyfishermen*

bass on the east coast of the USA, and sea-trout in the Baltic. Any of these will work for bass, but so will a simple reservoir lure like a Cat's Whisker or a Froggie. Beware, though, of rust – bronzed hooks will not survive for a second season. Leaders are uncomplicated – level 10 or 12lb B.S. monofilament, the length of your rod, will do the job nicely.

As to when to fish, an approach before low water enables one to see the bare bones of the area, noting gullies and structure before the tide hides all. The early stages of the flowing tide are a good time to fish, but always watch your rear and make sure that the tide is not creeping behind you, cutting off your retreat. Whatever the stage of the tide, dawn and dusk are great times to be on the water, and are peak feeding times for bass.

In good weather mullet are almost always visible around river-mouths and in estuaries. They are not so easy to catch and you may have to spend many hours before you find a killing method. This is one time you may find it advantageous to fish with two or three flies; a Diawl Bach is effective in some places, a Gammarus shrimp (or grayling bug) in others. Fishing a team lets you ring the changes. If you hook a 5lb mullet in shallow water you will probably regret listening to my advice to use a cheap reel!

A favourite of mine is the garfish. They can be plentiful in Welsh estuaries in the early summer, often visible swimming at the surface, sometimes splashing

Garfish
Easy to spot, but difficult to hook!

around clumps of floating weed. They investigate anything floating on the surface, including your flyline, often rolling or jumping over it, and will take any small baitfish imitation. Garfish can be quite difficult to hook - this is an occasion when I sometimes turn to a team of small bright wet-flies: Butcher; Teal, Blue and Silver; Red Tag and the like. And don't be too surprised if you hook a leaping sea-trout!

Other fish that you may take on the fly – mackerel, of course, and sometimes scad or horse mackerel; pollack and, more rarely, coalfish, over the rocks. In estuaries you may catch a flounder, but if you use weighted flies you will catch lesser weevers, so beware of grabbing any small fish that has taken your fly. A jab from a weever's spine could land you in hospital.

A fly-caught thick-lipped grey mullet
Arguably the ultimate flyfishing challenge

If one thing has revolutionised flyfishing in recent years - freshwater as well as salt - it is the introduction of lightweight chest waders. They give us access to places we could never get to in the days when all we had were rubber thigh boots. You can wet-wade, but usually only in the daytime. At dawn and dusk it is just too cold. Wet-wading or in waders – be careful. It is only too easy to find an apparently safe perch on a rock as the tide begins to make, only to find the water much deeper than you expected when you come to escape. I have had several scary moments that could easily have found me swimming for my life.

Scary moments and weever jabs aside, flyfishing in the sea is ideal for the angler holidaying on the Welsh coast. Unfettered by heavy tackle, just a few flies in his pocket and a rod in his hand, he can pop down to the shore first thing in the morning, or at dusk, with every chance of excellent sport."

Tackle care

Tackle is not accident-proof. For example, we've all had rod rests blown over by a rogue gust of wind, resulting in chipped or broken rod rings. Replace these immediately (your local tackle shop will often provide this service) as damaged rings are adept at fraying the line, leading to breakages and the need to replace your line as well. But the biggest enemy of shore angling tackle by far is the constantly-present salt water and its corrosive properties. You needn't drop a reel into the sea for this to become a problem: if fishing a good surf the flying spray will do the job just as effectively. Rinse reels in fresh water after a session and wipe down the rod with a damp cloth. Hooks will rust but are cheap – lures are expensive so give them a good rinse too, then leave rinsed items somewhere warm to dry out.

Reels need servicing periodically, an ideal time being the quiet period in February and March. If mechanically-minded, you might attempt this task yourself, with reference to the exploded parts diagram that comes with reels when purchased: alternatively get your reel serviced by a specialist. Servicing involves stripping-down, cleaning individual parts (it's amazing where sand grains can get), possibly using solvents in some cases, then thoroughly drying, greasing or oiling parts as required with special reel lubricants then reassembling. It's a good opportunity to check too for excessive wear in any parts that can be replaced before they completely seize up on you halfway through a fishing session.

Cameras

Like many anglers, I like to keep a photographic record of my trips and catches and there is a wealth of choice out there when it comes to equipment. Most of my photography though concerns weather and landscapes and for these shoots I use a Nikon D300 DSLR. Such cameras can represent significant investments and given the harsh physical environment that the coast presents, with sand and salt spray getting everywhere, one has to be ultra careful. Smaller compact digital cameras are a lot cheaper – they may vary in quality with respect to landscape-photography, but one thing they tend to have in common is the ability to take good sharp close-up images in 'macro' setting. Online and magazine reviews, of which there are many, will point you in the right direction. The Pentax Optio E35 that I used for the fish images when I did not have the Nikon to hand has done an admirable job. Compacts are surprisingly tough too – my E35 was dropped over the side of Aberystwyth Stone Jetty on one occasion, bouncing down the well-spaced-out concrete ledges and coming to rest, Italian Job-style, half-on and half-off the last step above the water. I scrambled down to retrieve it and was amazed to find it still worked perfectly well.

Modern digital cameras auto-focus and shoot in a matter of seconds – the important thing is to learn to compose equally quickly (unless your fish is going to be eaten, when you should dispatch it first before doing anything else). Keep the camera pre-set to macro, compose, shoot and get the fish back in the water. When focusing, digital cameras are looking for areas where colour or brightness change abruptly. At night, therefore, a useful trick to aid focusing is to shine your torch on a high-contrast part of the fish such as a dark dorsal fin against pale sand. A further useful tip is to shoot a larger field of view than you will need – this reduces time spent in composing and you can always crop images using your photographic software at leisure, once you are back in the warm.

If using a DSLR, keep it in a well-constructed camera case – I carry my case on my person and it doesn't get in the way. Doing so is better than keeping it in a tackle box, where if you are really unlucky a rogue wave might drench it in salt water.

Once home, let any moisture dry and go around the camera with a fine, clean paintbrush to remove any sand – this is especially important with the lens. You will of course have a UV filter over the lens as a cheap barrier to salty spray, but before you take a lens cloth to the lens itself, get every last grain of sand out of the way, or a wipe will leave it scratched. The one advantage with compact cameras is that they can be stowed in a chest pocket – just make sure it is buttoned-up if you don't want to repeat my experience at Aberystwyth.

SOURCING BAIT

The marine food chain is a long and complicated one. Fish eat all manner of things, from microscopic plankton and copepods (tiny crustaceans) that are the staple diets of herrings through to large fish and seals that are the prey of choice of the larger sharks. Within this broad spectrum we find the baits that are most commonly used by anglers, because they are easy to obtain and because they are proven fish catchers. Many of Cardigan Bay's coastal towns have tackle and fish shops where baits can be purchased, including, in season, fresh worms, crabs and mackerel. Tackle shops also carry a good range of frozen baits. Gathering your own can be a lot less reliable and is time consuming. Those of us living on or near to the coast can take advantage of things that are not so easily available to a visiting angler. For example, a furious winter's gale may wash hundreds of shellfish such as razors ashore, to be picked, bagged and frozen down by locals – if the gulls

Clams after a storm
After a big gale, local anglers can pick up shellfish washing ashore – if the gulls don't get there first

haven't eaten them first. Or a rare early heat wave in March might bring on the first moult of the shore crabs. These are things of which only those living within striking distance can regularly take advantage.

What to look for

Let's have a look at the baits commonly supplied fresh or frozen from the tackle shops, applying first principles. Baits work by two properties – scent and sight – and sometimes both in combination. At night, or in rough, heavily-coloured seas, scent is key, and a bait without scent is extremely unlikely to create the slightest bit of interest. To begin with of course, all baits have scent, but once plonked out there in the surf and tide it is soon washed out of them. Therefore, baits have to be regularly changed. How often? Some match anglers will change baits strictly every 15 minutes, but they are often using very small baits such as tiny ragworms. For more typically-sized baits, this can be extended to 20 or 30 minutes (so long as there are not armies of crabs busy stripping the hooks) and large baits like mackerel heads will be giving off a good scent trail for much

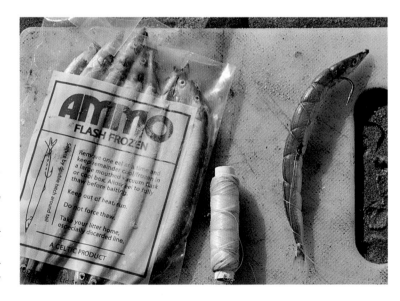

Frozen sandeel
A frozen sandeel, carefully mounted using bait elastic, works by both scent and sight when the underwater visibility is good

Squid and sandeel
A squid-sandeel wrap is a scent-based bait that is resistant to the attention of crabs

longer than that. I'm generally happy with half an hour before I refresh my bait. By day, sight also plays a part which is why baits fished in the day aimed at predatory fish in clear water conditions need to look reasonably lifelike – a sandeel fished whole and carefully presented will catch far more predators than one that has been folded over with the hook through it several times and looking like the marine equivalent of road kill.

Sandeels also work well as scent-based baits for fish that do a lot of scavenging in gloomy conditions. Over rough or mixed ground, their relatively soft flesh soon succumbs to the relentless attacks of crabs. A good trick under such circumstances is to have a pack of frozen squid in the bait bucket – if a squid is opened up and cleaned its white flesh may be rolled around the sandeel and hook shank before being bound tight with bait elastic. This serves to protect the sandeel from the crabs to an extent and is known as a squid-sandeel wrap.

Oily fish like mackerel, herrings and the imported Pacific sauries (also called blueys) are great scent baits that will take many species, with the target fish determining the size of bait, of course. Fresh or blast-frozen mackerel and herring strips are fairly tough and only need securing with bait elastic if long-range power casting is required – but blueys are relatively soft and binding is recommended. For sight feeders, long, thin strips cut from the silver-white bellies of mackerel or herring are most effective. Small slivers of the same flesh are often used to 'tip-off' scented baits such as lugworms – the fish being drawn in generally by the scent and then homing in when they spot the bright tip waving about enticingly in the surf. Small thin strips of squid also work in the same way.

Lugworms are sold fresh in some places but are more commonly available frozen. Anglers recognise two kinds: the common, brown or 'blow' lug which does not freeze well (but which can be very good used fresh) and the larger black lugworm which freezes excellently and is thus purchased from the tackle shop freezer. Black lug are liquorice-black and their leathery skin is tough enough to withstand crab activity for a time. They can be used whole, threaded up the hook and line, often with a second hook rigged in tandem in case a fish attacks from the 'wrong' end, or cut into sections to attract smaller species like flatfish. After storms in autumn and winter, lugworms work well in combination with shellfish, as the waves will have washed these out of the inshore sandbanks and the fish will be expecting to find and feed on them. Of the shellfish baits, razor is the most readily available and a proven catcher. Again, bait elastic ensures good presentation and prevents the bait disintegrating during the cast. An alternative is to defrost the razors, shell them and refreeze the meat with half a handful of salt. The moisture will be drawn out and the bait will be much tougher. This trick also works for leftover sandeels after a summer day's pollack fishing – salted, they become leathery and work well cut into sections for winter whiting.

Live ragworm, sold by many tackle shops, catches a variety of species but is especially effective around breakwaters – maybe because the varied fish that inhabit such popular places are so used to eating it. It, and its smaller cousin, the harbour ragworm (also known plurally as 'maddies'), are also effective when fished close-in on surf beaches for flounders, bass

Frozen mackerel

Frozen mackerel takes a wide range of species: small strips may be cut from the fillets or they can be used whole for large predators – as can the head and guts

A SELECTION OF READILY AVAILABLE BAITS

Bluey

Blueys are excellent scent-based baits, but use bait elastic to secure the strips to your hook

Frozen mackerel

Small thin strips of mackerel belly are effective when float fished for predators who readily mistake them for fry

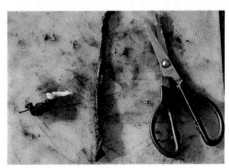

Black Lugworm

Small slivers of mackerel (or squid) can also be used to tip-off scent-based baits such as black lugworm

Lugworm and shellfish

Lugworm also works well as a 'cocktail' with shellfish such as razor

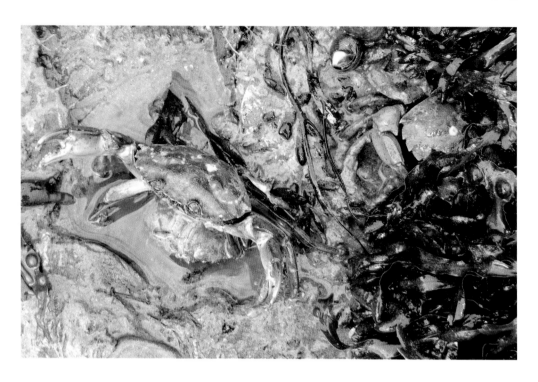

Crabs

Crabs only mate after they have moulted. The one hiding in the seaweed is a recently-mated soft crab

and other species. That different baits suit different types of venues at different times of year is an important principle that will be explored in the sections on the different types of ground and fish species found around the Bay.

Crabs are excellent bait for many species, but only when they 'peel'. Like all arthropods, their exoskeleton is rigid and of a fixed size so that a growing crab has to moult once or more times a year. This is the peel and it coincides with mating time too. The ordinary (or hardback), crab finds a suitable hidey-hole and changes occur to its shell, which fades in colour and becomes brittle. This is known as a peeler crab. The shell is then cast off, legs and all, as the crab takes in water and swells in size. At this stage the new shell is as soft as jelly and the crab is known as a soft back or 'softie'. The shell then starts to harden, feeling papery at first then eventually rock hard. Hardback crabs used as bait take few species (although many fish are caught with them in their guts), whereas peelers and softies are deadly. Size of bait is determined by the fish

3333333

species targeted – if fishing for large bass, a whole crab is often used. It is first killed then peeled if it still has the old shell, and then cut into two or more pieces to maximise scent output and, being soft, securely bound onto the hook with elastic. Bind the legs towards the eye of the hook and the fish will tend to take from the hook point end, thus ensuring an optimum ratio of fish hooked to bites.

For foragers, brown lugworm beds (with occasional white ragworm) do exist in some of the estuaries, although many have been overexploited in the past and are not what they were. Please backfill any excavations made – having checked first that digging is permitted. Black lugworms occur on some beaches but not commonly – they are only accessible on low spring tides. Harbour rag can be found by squelching about in the mud of some harbours at low tide. Peeler and soft crabs are present in rocky and weedy areas during the warmer months, as are prawns. The crabs hide under the weed and rocks, but please, please, carefully replace any rocks you look under properly. Too often, I come across weed covered boulders that have been heaved over and left on their backs – the weed all rotting and the little ecosystem wrecked and useless as a future crab lurking place. Shellfish are widespread but most species are only available on the bigger tides at low water. An exception is the mussel, which is common in some estuaries, but which is not used by many anglers: its softness makes it difficult to fish with, though shelling and salting, as described above with razors, toughens it up nicely. In season, mackerel may be caught in many areas provided that the weather is settled.

Thus, visiting anglers have a potentially wide range of baits available to them via a bit of gathering and a bit of purchasing. Supporting the local tackle shop also serves another important purpose – it helps it stay in business, which is important to local communities, and means that when you travel down here only to find you have left all your hooks at home, there will still be somewhere left open to help you out.

One of the most enjoyable bait collecting experiences that I have had took place many years ago, during an awful year in which many fish species failed to show up in numbers. Quantities of mackerel were so dismal that the Aberystwyth charter fleet were left at the end of the year with empty bait freezers. Frozen mackerel is a mainstay bait for early season tope and bream fishing, and in order to get around the problem, local skippers purchased a drift net with herrings the intended target. Some of the regular local crews helped out: we would leave the harbour at sunset in late autumn, motor out for a mile or two, cut the engine, deploy the net and drift north for a couple of hours with the flooding tide, fishing for whiting to bide away the time until the haul-in. It was a hit-and-miss business, but on one particular clear, moonlit night the net was hauled back in and a myriad of herrings appeared as a carpet of metallic silver on the sea surface – an amazing sight that must have been familiar a century or two ago, when Aberystwyth was an important herring port. The freezers were filled, all was well and the two herrings I fried in oatmeal later that evening made one of the best meals I have ever had, before or since. It has always amazed me that herring is not more popular – it's the only fish I actually buy for eating, and it is one of the cheapest and tastiest available.

The forces that shape the marine environment of Cardigan Bay

All outdoor activities have their viability on any given day strongly influenced by the weather, and shore angling is no exception. Indeed, at some fishing venues the weather will determine whether they are even safe to venture upon. Other venues are safe in most kinds of weather but in certain conditions are completely unproductive. Let's have a run through the various weather types and highlight those to avoid.

Wind

Wind is a major factor. The only venues that are relatively unaffected by high winds are estuaries, but even then, fishing in a Force 8 gale is plain miserable – sand gets everywhere, your rod rest keeps blowing over and anything not nailed down goes flapping away. Wind speeds are measured on the Beaufort Scale, which goes from Force 0 (calm), to Force 12 (hurricane, 73mph and over). In Cardigan Bay, the prevailing south-westerly winds are onshore along many parts of the coast. Onshore winds of Force 2 to Force 4 (4mph to 17mph), that bring up a good steady surf, are ideal for beach fishing and force 4 is the absolute limit of safety when fishing rock-ledges and breakwaters. Force 5 to Force 6 starts to create too heavy a sea on the open coast but the estuaries will offer a viable alternative. When winds of Force 7 and above are forecast it's better to stay home. During the autumn and winter storms, winds are often Gale Force 8 or more and in occasional instances can top Violent Storm Force 11 (64mph to 72mph).

Beaufort values describe steady winds over several minutes: in such powerful storms individual, short-lived gusts will be substantially stronger. These severe storms can bring major changes to venues, gouging gullies along beaches, ripping up offshore sandbanks and eroding dunes and cliffs.

Offshore winds are widely regarded as poor for fishing. There's an old saying that goes 'when the wind's in the east, the fish bite the least'. In my experience it's true – once an easterly gets above about Force 3, the fishing almost always dies right off. Many reasons have been suggested for this – one possibility that I favour is that a prolonged offshore wind affects the drift of food items, which move offshore with the fish following. Another possibility (in winter and spring anyway) is that easterlies tend to bring with them very cold air that chills the sands and shallows harshly over low tide, when the sea is already at its coldest. The fact that some easterlies are associated with high pressure may have a bearing, too, some say – but I'm not convinced about that: I've caught well when the pressure is high and the wind is coming from other directions. Easterlies will certainly kill the surf dead, unless there is a big ground swell running – when the spray from the breaking waves will blow back seaward in spectacular fashion.

THE BEAUFORT SCALE

Force	Wind Speed (mph)	Description	Sea Condition
0	0	Calm	Sea like a mirror
1	1 – 3	Light air	Ripples but without foam crests
2	4 – 7	Light breeze	Small wavelets. Crests do not break
3	8 – 12	Gentle breeze	Large wavelets. Perhaps scattered white horses
4	13 – 17	Moderate breeze	Small waves. Fairly frequent white horses
5	18 – 24	Fresh breeze	Moderate waves. Many white horses
6	25 – 30	Strong breeze	Large waves begin to form; white foam crests. Probably spray
7	31 – 38	Near gale	Sea heaps up and white foam blown in streaks along the direction of the wind
8	39 – 46	Gale	Moderately high waves. Crests begin to break into spindrift. The foam is blown in well-marked streaks along the direction of the wind
9	47 – 54	Severe gale	High waves. Dense foam along the direction of the wind. Crests of waves begin to roll over. Spray may affect visibility
10	55 – 63	Storm	Very high waves with long overhanging crests. The surface of the sea takes a white appearance. The tumbling of the sea becomes heavy and shock-like. Visibility affected
11	64 – 72	Violent storm	Exceptionally high waves. The sea is completely covered with long white patches of foam lying in the direction of the wind. Visibility affected
12	73+	Hurricane	The air is filled with foam and spray. Sea completely white with driving spray. Visibility very seriously affected

Swells

Groundswells are long wavelength waves that originate far out to sea. Generated by severe storms out in the mid-Atlantic, they roll their way across the ocean to slam into the coast one after another – even if there is no wind locally. Once a swell reaches 3ft or so, the energy of the breakers generated along shallow beaches will push the fish out into deeper water to avoid exhaustion and in addition fishing on rocks and breakwaters becomes dangerous – and progressively so, because the greater the swell the greater the danger, so that eventually other marks such as steep shingle beaches become dodgy, too. Exceptionally, swells in Cardigan Bay can exceed 15ft and on big tides these can be damaging as the huge, surging waves at high tide can top sea defences. The good news is that there are swell forecast pages online, aimed at surfers, but they can also provide vital information for the angler deciding whether to go out or not. Along the open coast I strictly avoid swells of over 3ft and would advise others to do the same. In reality, this does not mean that much fishing time is lost, as generally swells stay below this size. The important thing is not to get caught out when the relevant information is so readily accessed.

Swells
A large groundswell and an offshore wind in combination at Tywyn's South Beach: impressive, but hopeless for fishing

Rain and thunderstorms

Rain is not normally a problem to fishing on beaches (unless you have a compulsive aversion to getting wet). However prolonged rainy weather which dumps huge amounts of water over the Welsh mountains can kill the fishing for a while by flooding the estuaries with fresh water and diluting the seawater along the nearby coast. Many fish have low tolerance to such abrupt changes in salinity and they move out into deeper water for a few days until the tides flush out the fresh water. The Environment Agency's Flood Warnings service can tell you if such a rainfall has occurred, as it will issue flood warnings on the rivers draining the mountains. Rain on rock marks is another matter altogether as it tends to make the rock lethally slippery. Such places really are fair-weather venues.

Thunderstorm
A thunderstorm just starting off Borth Beach. If you haven't packed up already, do so immediately

Thunderstorms occur all year round in Wales but are infrequent. They can develop when squally westerlies blow in with lots of sharp but short-lived showers, or when northerlies bring snow showers in winter, or when hot, sultry summer heatwaves break down – hence the term 'thundery breakdown' sometimes heard in summer weather forecasts. These big summer storms are typically the most active in terms of lightning discharges. The effect that any thunderstorm has on fishing is to make it a potentially lethal activity. Modern beach rods generally contain carbon fibre, which is an excellent lightning conductor. If thunder is forecast, postpone the trip. If caught out, pack up and leave straight away before the storm arrives. If unconvinced by that, consider for a moment that the temperature of a lightning bolt exceeds that of the surface of

Squalls
Two anglers caught out in a blinding squall – the definition of misery

the sun, and that being killed outright by one may be better than the awful complications that some survivors may face. Take lightning seriously. Squally conditions with heavy showers are generally too rough to fish in any case.

Temperatures

Both heat and cold can sometimes have adverse effects on the fishing. Prolonged hot weather along shallow coastlines can lead to blooms of planktonic algae which use up a lot of the oxygen in the water. This affects the fish and they move out into deeper, cooler water until the problem has passed. Because this problem is especially common in late spring, it is often referred to as 'May weed' or 'May water' and, due to the colouration that the organisms give to the water, 'red tides'. Such blooms typically lead to pungent smells and copious foam washing ashore in unusual quantities, so they tend to be fairly obvious. Once the foam turns a dull dark-brown, meaning that the planktonic algae is dying-off, the end is in sight and as a general rule the fishing will improve within a few days.

Cold conditions that have many anglers taking up knitting as an alternative still produce catches, but severe frosts of

-10°C and below chill the sand at low tide, which then cools the water on the following flood tide and these conditions put off fish and anglers alike. The same problem can occur in spring, when sea temperatures are low in any case. A series of chilly nights, the sort that worry gardeners, can kill the fishing stone dead until the weather warms up again. Chilly nights in autumn though have a less pronounced effect as the sea is at its peak in its annual temperature cycle. Deeper water is less affected by temperature extremes, so hot or cold conditions are still fine for most rock marks. As such venues typically involve a strenuous approach, take plenty of water with you on hot days as dehydration is most unpleasant, and may be downright dangerous. As is sunburn – a high protection factor sun cream (SPF 30 or higher) will stop your skin getting microwaved by the UVA and UVB rays coming down from the sun above and back up from the reflective surface of the water.

Ice
Ice floes on the Dyfi Estuary during the bitter weather of December 2010. If you fish when it is this cold you are very unlikely to catch anything but hypothermia

Forecasting for yourself

If the weather interests you, it will very much benefit your fishing career if you learn how to forecast conditions yourself. Because I became interested in weather photography and what in the USA is known as storm chasing, I got into forecasting about ten years ago, and it was, and continues to be, one hell of an education. There is a wealth of forecast charts (known as 'Model Output') available on the internet, from basic things like temperature and wind through to more complex ones like instability and wind-shear – essential for severe thunderstorm forecasting. Because we Brits love talking about the weather, there is a choice of several internet forums that offer the opportunity to learn an awful lot from experienced amateur and professional forecasters alike. What I've learned has without doubt helped my fishing no end – it is very rarely that I get caught out by anything unexpected these days, whereas twenty years ago it was not uncommon.

I recall one occasion back then, when a girlfriend and I were walking out across the half mile of flat sand to an estuary mark, on an evening when there were a few heavy showers around. Nearing the water, I suddenly became aware of a most unusual sensation. It felt as though my beard was moving about on its own. At the same time, my girlfriend was seized by fits of laughter. On my enquiring as to what was so funny, she pointed at me, or more specifically my hair. I've always had long hair but in this instance it was completely stood up on end. The static electricity levels must have been phenomenal. At that point the penny dropped rather quickly and we jogged back to our transport as fast as wellies would allow. The vicious thunderstorms that followed continued for the entire night.

Tides

Understanding the tides is another essential prerequisite for a successful shore angler. Tides are caused by the twin gravitational pulls of the moon and, to about half as much extent, of the sun, on the surface of the Earth as it rotates on its axis. The gravitational force maintains an extensive bulge in the sea surface that travels around with a return period of a little over twelve hours. Thus, if high tide at Aberystwyth is at six o'clock one morning, the next high tide will be at about half-past six that evening. In between these highs, there will be low tide. Along the Cardigan Bay coast, the tidal flow from high to low water (known as the ebb) runs north to south in most places. The incoming tide (the flood) runs the opposite way – south to north. As a result, high tide at Cardigan, in the south of the bay, will be about half an hour before that at Aberystwyth, whilst Barmouth, to the north, will see high tide about half an hour later again. The flood is a slightly faster current than the ebb, and along the central Cardigan Bay coast the flood lasts for about five and a half hours, the ebb for about seven hours. At full high and full low tides, there is no flow, and these relatively brief periods are known as slack water.

Tides vary in size according to where the moon is in the sky with regard to the sun. Twice a month, at new moon and full moon, the moon, sun and Earth are in a straight line and the gravitational pull is at its greatest, so the tides are large. These are called spring tides – not because they occur in spring (they occur all year round) but because they come (spring up) quickly. When the moon is at first quarter or third quarter, the combined effect is at its weakest and the tides are small – these are known as neap tides. The term is thought to be derived from an Old English word 'nep' meaning 'becoming lower'.

In considering the tides, there are also differences in the distance between the moon and the Earth to take into account. When the moon is closest to the Earth (at perigee), the biggest spring tides occur. When it is furthest from the Earth (at

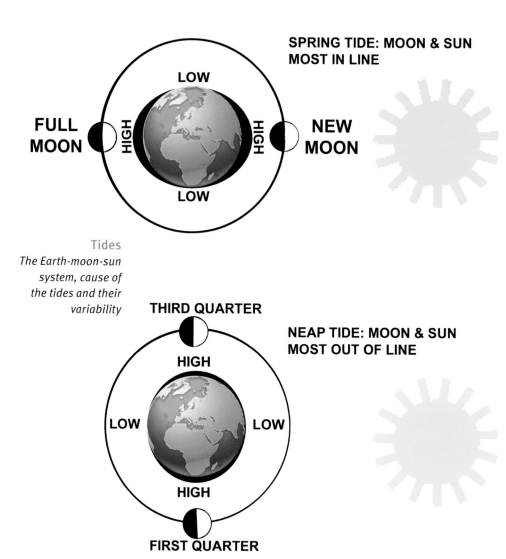

SPRING TIDE: MOON & SUN
MOST IN LINE

LOW

FULL
MOON

HIGH

HIGH

NEW
MOON

LOW

Tides
The Earth-moon-sun
system, cause of
the tides and their
variability

THIRD QUARTER

NEAP TIDE: MOON & SUN
MOST OUT OF LINE

HIGH

LOW

LOW

HIGH

FIRST QUARTER

apogee), the smallest spring tides occur. A book of tide tables (an essential and cheap item) will detail these, generally giving the tidal heights in metres. For example, looking through the tide tables for 2011 for Aberystwyth reveals the biggest spring tides of the year of 5.7m (18.7ft) to occur in February/March and August/September. The smallest ones of 4.6m (15.1ft) are in November/December and May/June. A 3ft difference does not sound a lot but on a shallow sandy beach it can make a big difference – just think how far out you have to wade on such beaches to be in three feet of water. That's how much further out the tide will be at slack low on a perigee spring tide. Neap tides can be as small as 3.2m (10.5ft), when, as a consequence, much of the sand remains underwater at low tide and at high tide the water barely laps at the feet of the beachhead shingle.

Because there are such height differences between spring and neap tides, it follows that in spring tides a much greater volume of water moves through than during neaps. The result of this is that the tidal flow is at its greatest, on flood or ebb, during the biggest tides and at its weakest on the smallest neaps. Fish, never being creatures to waste energy, take advantage of this, so that spring tides are periods of seasonal migration. At low tide on springs, the waterline is so much lower down the beach that it may bring productive feeding areas within casting range. If rough weather on one peak spring tide throws up a lot of seaweed onto the strand line, there will then be a fortnight of smaller tides as the cycle goes down to neap and back up again. During that period, the seaweed will start to decompose and the countless maggots of seaweed flies will hatch out and start eating it. If the next peak spring tide washes weed, maggots and all back into the sea again, the fish will move in to take advantage of an easy feast. Such things may be anticipated and taken advantage of.

These effects alone hint at spring tides being better for fishing in most places, although this is not an absolute rule. Some estuaries fish better on neaps – they might dry out too much at low water on springs or at high water the sea might top the deep channels flooding acres of shallow flats and making the channels inaccessible. Likewise, in some rocky areas, where the tidal flows are always much stronger, neaps may offer the best chance of fishing with baits on the seabed without rigs getting swept up into snags all the time.

Which is best, flood or ebb?

That is a frequently-asked question and the answer varies from location to location. Over shallow ground, on a big spring the tide can go out so quickly that fish can risk death from getting stranded as the waves recede. A friend of mine illustrated this point a year or two ago when, during a beach walk, he found a decent-sized turbot flapping about on the sand near the water's edge. At some deep water rock marks, the ebb might be gentle but the flood rips through making it impossible to hold ground, even with a heavy sinker. But lures are effective in riptides – it's just a case of matching tactics to suit the conditions. On beaches that strip a long way with the ebb, it is traditional to arrive an hour or two before low water and then fish the tide up. There is more than just habit to this – it gives you chance to see the beach uncovered, so you can look for any features like gullies or clumps of weedy boulders that might either hold fish or alternatively, snag your line later in the session when the tide is well in. But once you know a beach fairly well you can fish any part of a tide aware of such details already.

Away from the rips around the headlands and the estuaries on full ebb or flood, very strong tides are uncommon in Cardigan Bay. However, some beaches do feature a lateral flow, most noticeable on spring tides. If you cast straight out and your line starts bowing out one way or the other, and there's no side-wind to blame for this, reel back in and walk up-tide a little – for example if the tide is pulling your line from right to left facing out to sea, walk to the right 20 or 30 yards, wade out and cast. Then wade straight back in and walk back down to your rod rest and tighten the line – the bow of line that then forms will point from your rod tip straight out to sea. In such situations use breakout-style leads to grip the seabed.

———— THE FISHING GROUNDS ————

How Cardigan Bay was formed – a quick geological interlude

In order to understand the variety of ground available to the sea angler around Cardigan Bay, it is instructive to take a quick look at the Bay's history over the past 18,000 years. This sounds like a long time, although when one ponders the fact that the rocky outcrops around the Bay are hundreds of millions of years old, it doesn't feel so bad.

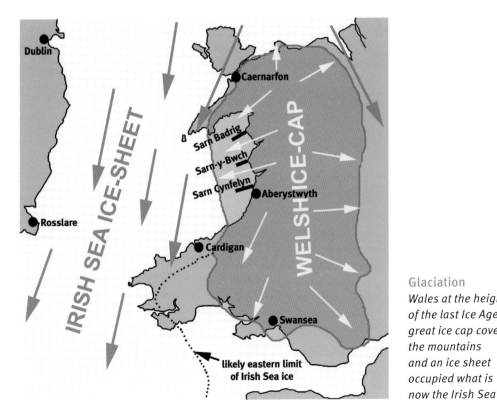

Glaciation
Wales at the height of the last Ice Age. A great ice cap covered the mountains and an ice sheet occupied what is now the Irish Sea

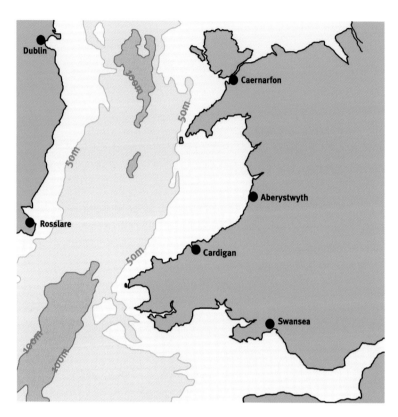

Underwater topography
Sea depths in the Irish Sea only locally exceed 100m: this is relevant when one considers that global sea level rise as the ice melted exceeded 120m

Eighteen thousand years ago, we were still in the depths of the last Ice Age. Great ice caps sat over the Welsh mountains and valley glaciers descended from them, across the lowlands to feed the main Irish Sea ice sheet. In other words, the landscape was unrecognisable – and uninhabitable. But as the climate recovered over the next few thousand years, the ice melted away, retreating back to the higher mountains and the polar regions of the planet. As a direct consequence of all that melting of ice, global sea levels rose by nearly 400ft (or 120m), drowning the extensive lowlands that fringed the Welsh mountains under shallow waters – and Cardigan Bay came into being.

Anybody who has been to a glaciated mountain range like the Alps, or has watched a documentary about the Himalayas, will have noticed the tremendous quantities of rocky debris that glaciers rip away and push along with them – anything from grains of sand up to great boulders. The same thing occurred here in Cardigan Bay – as the glaciers made their way down from the mountains they dumped countless billions of tons of material onto the lowland plains. As the ice retreated, this great expanse of debris was then channelled by melt-water rivers and finally reworked by the waves of the rising sea into extensive banks of sand and gravel, interrupted by large, elongated mounds of boulders, these marking the lateral moraines along the sides of the former valley glaciers.

By about 7000 years ago, the rate of sea level rise had slowed down – to the extent that coastal woodlands and peat bogs were able to form and last a few centuries. The so-called 'submerged forests' of Borth and elsewhere, visible at low tide, mark this development. About 3000 years ago, the sea, having overwhelmed these ancient woodlands, reached its peak post-glacial level. During this whole long period of sea level rise, the annual rate averaged out at some 9mm per year, although there were periods during which the waters rose more quickly. The aptly-named Meltwater Pulse 1A, 14,600 to

Drowned landscape
The Fossil Forest on Borth Beach. Sea levels were a lot lower several thousand years ago and are now rising again

13,500 years ago, saw an estimated rise of between 1.4 and 2.1 cm per year. In recent decades, the process has restarted and currently the sea is rising by about 3mm per year as a consequence of climate change. Whether this continues, slows down or gets worse, is within the power of Mankind to address – if ignored, parts of this book may require extensive revision by the year 2200!

As a consequence of the dumping and reworking of all that glacial debris, and despite the large rise in sea levels that occurred as the glaciers retreated, much of central and northern Cardigan Bay is rather shallow. Within a nautical mile of the coast, it is rarely more than 15-30ft deep. The 60ft submarine contour is about ten nautical miles out from the coast. Locally, there are much deeper inshore features which are the remains of old, drowned river valleys, such as Muddy Hollow in Tremadog Bay and The Gutter to the south-west of Aberystwyth. The large, elongated mounds of boulders left behind by the glaciers form much shallower reefs – the well-known Sarnau. On low spring tides, even a few nautical miles off the coast, the water over these 'causeways', as they are known to local boatmen, may in places be only a few feet deep. For this reason, the western end of each of the three largest Sarnau reefs is marked by a large navigational buoy to warn mariners of the hazard.

A drastic change is to be found towards the Bay's north-western and south-western extremities, where much deeper waters are frequently found. Off the south-west part of the Llŷn Peninsula and off the Pembrokeshire coast, there are points where it is possible to cast from rock platforms into as much as 100ft of water. In these areas, what were once rocky hills, standing out from the lowland plain, are now submerged reefs and even islands, such as Bardsey and Ramsey.

The main valleys that drain the Welsh mountains, such as the Dyfi, were carved out to a great depth by the glaciers of the Ice Age. As sea levels rose, they became silted-up, so that water depths of a few metres at most are now typical in our

The Causeway
*The bouldery reef
of Sarn Cynfelyn,
an ancient glacial
moraine, at low tide.
It extends as a rough
undersea ridge for a
further 6.5 nautical
miles from the coast*

estuaries, although their entrances are often guarded by even shallower sandbars – Aberdyfi Bar is a notorious example. Waves and tides continue to rework the debris left behind by the glaciers, supplemented by sand, silt and mud fed into the bay by the main rivers draining the mountains. The sediment supply is also added to by the thousands of tonnes of rock that falls from the cliffs every year as rain, frost, wind and waves slowly erode them landwards. Many centuries of such cliff erosion have led, in places, to the formation of shallow, rocky reefs, covered over at high tide but which can be extensive at low water.

Low-lying, shallow stretches of coast typically consist of sandy surf beaches alternating with tracts of bouldery mixed ground. The sandy beaches uncover for a long way out over low water, especially on spring tides, and are usually backed by coarse shingle along the high water mark, often with a hinterland of sand dunes. Conversely, along the rougher sections of coast there are much steeper shingle beaches, where the flat sand may not uncover over low water.

Thus have the forces of nature conspired, over the past 18,000 years, to bring about this excellent variety of fishing grounds. Their legacy is a wide range of fishing options, only dependant upon season, fish sought after, weather conditions and the stamina of the angler.

The different fishing grounds and how to fish them

The fishing grounds of Cardigan Bay are, for the purposes of this book, divided into seven categories, comprising shallow sandy beaches, steep shingle beaches, mixed ground, shallow reefs, deep water rock marks, estuaries and man-made structures. This interesting variety of fishing potential does not, however, enjoy a simple, uniform distribution – each section of coast has its own characteristics. The concave shape of the Bay is a major factor, because it determines how exposed any section of coastline is to the prevailing south-westerly wind. Let's examine the different types of ground, before embarking on a tour around the coast which will give anglers, and especially visitors, an idea of what sort of fishing to expect depending upon where they are.

Shallow sandy beaches

Anglers visiting central and northern Cardigan Bay are spoiled for choice when it comes to such beaches. A lot of anglers prefer them to other venues because they are so easy to fish – apart from anything else, snags are generally rare. Although they can at first sight look rather featureless, they are in fact teeming with life – it's just that most of it lives beneath the surface of the sand, and the closer down to the low water mark you get, the more of it there is.

Sand has that useful property of looseness, which allows things to burrow down into it: shrimps, crabs, worms, bivalves and fish like sandeels all take advantage of this. So what brings the fish in to feed? Either they are feeding on things that have left the sand of their own free will for some purpose or they are taking advantage of rough seas that have swept away the sandy cover, leaving the prey species at the mercy of surf and current. So here's the first critical point. These beaches are very weather dependent.

Sea conditions on such beaches range from flat calms to raging storms. They are generally thought of as surf beaches, meaning that no surf equals no fish. However, this isn't entirely true. In calm conditions, down below the low water mark, the filter-feeders like worms and bivalves will be feeding and visible to any passing fish. Sandeels will be swimming around (watch the terns diving for them on a sunny afternoon) and predators will be waiting in ambush. At first light the sandeels emerge from their cover and at dusk they burrow back into it. During such times they are even more vulnerable to attack. By day, in fine weather, the sea will often be full of swimmers and water sports enthusiasts, disturbing everything, but as night falls they head off home. So pick an evening or early morning tide, with low water falling in the middle of your session and get the baits out there. Bait-wise, think of what the fish are looking for – worms, shellfish and sandeels.

What species can you expect? You'll find both fish eaters such as rays, dogfish and turbot, and worm/shellfish eaters such as flounders and dabs. Bass will be present for much of the year and will take fish, worm and shellfish baits alike, being an opportunistic species. In the autumn, hordes of whiting invade the inshore waters and these add to the possibilities – but pick a big tide and fish over high water as they seem to prefer some depth of water over them. The best conditions for most species are when a decent surf is running. By decent I mean a short, choppy sea driven by wind rather than swell, with a force 2 to 4 onshore wind perfect. That will create a band of breaking waves about 100 yards out, with a series of foaming water-tables continually heading ashore from them in which the fish will be feeding. In stronger winds, when the surf seems to start about a quarter of a mile out, the fish will be far more dispersed. Likewise in calms, when long casting can be an advantage as the fish, without a surf to focus upon, will be hunting over a wide area. The worst conditions of all are when a huge swell is running, wind or no wind. This creates such powerful breakers that the fish have to expend more energy to stay in the right area than they can get by feeding. Quite sensibly, they move out a little until conditions have eased. A big swell is the one thing that is pretty much a kiss-of-death for fishing on such beaches.

A decent surf will fish well by day (dull weather best) or by night. To avoid the disturbance due to swimmers and surfers on the busier beaches, many anglers choose the night tides for the peace and quiet. Both incoming and outgoing tides can be productive, and with sufficient supplies of coffee a whole tidal cycle can be fished overnight if you pick your times carefully. The bigger spring tides fish best although neaps will still produce a few fish. Surf conditions are far more important than size of tide.

Casting distance required depends on species, but anglers new to such a venue are often surprised just how close-in some species will come in the right conditions. On some occasions, I have watched anglers wading out past the feeding zone in order to cast. A range of 30 to 50 yards is often quite enough. If you don't feel comfortable with that, then why not bring two rods and fish one close in and the other at your preferred range?

Such fishing is best in late spring, early summer and all of autumn, weather permitting. The midsummer months are often quieter. This may be due to several reasons – often, decent surf is less of a feature than it is in the spring and autumn months. Also, the sheer abundance of food just offshore in midsummer – when the mackerel shoals are messily chomping up billions of whitebait – will attract all sorts of fish to either clear up the mess left behind or, in the case of bass, chomp up a few mackerel instead. Thirdly, in the inshore shallows, algal blooms can occur in the summer months. As previously mentioned these can lower the oxygen levels of the water and any fish wishing to stay healthy will head out into deeper water.

From September right through to March, the north-western coasts of Europe see periods of stormy weather every year as big Atlantic lows roll in. Winds as high as force 10 or more, big swells and spring tides combine to do untold destruction to the sandbanks below the low water mark, normally untouched by the waves. Such conditions are completely unfishable, of course, but when the weather has calmed down, a food bonanza becomes available to the fish. Worms, shellfish such as razors and all sorts of clams will have been torn from their sandy lairs and will wash ashore where, if you are quick enough, you can beat the gulls and gather a few to be deep frozen for bait. Some of the shellfish will have been smashed by the storm waves against the shingle or groynes, releasing bits of flesh to the sea, and once conditions settle then the fish will be moving in for an easy feed.

Such post-storm periods are when shellfish baits really come into their own. They will be taken by most species depending on hook and bait size. In such circumstances, fishing from low tide up is especially advantageous as it will allow a good examination of the beach – look for things like gullies, pebbly depressions or scoured-out holes at the ends of groynes. Food will collect preferentially in such areas as the tide comes in and covers them, making them fish-attracting features and therefore ideal targets to cast into.

There is one problem that can occur after a blow, though – weed. Floating weed is always present in the bay, but after a storm the sea may be full of the stuff. There is nothing more disheartening than getting up at three in the morning, driving miles to the beach, getting your weatherproof kit on, baiting up and casting out only, after a few moments, to see the rod tip start to nod rhythmically as each successive breaker tugs at the weed caught on the line. Pumping a mass of weed back is in itself an arm-wrenching affair and unearthing your rig from the stubborn, tangled mass of stems and fronds can take ten minutes or more. Such conditions are frankly a waste of time. So how can they be avoided?

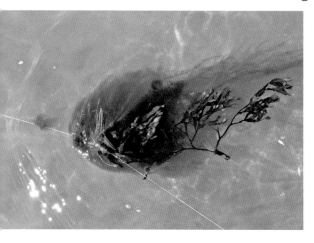

The shore anglers' bane

Floating seaweed readily snags on fishing line and will tend to bunch up around the knot joining the leader to the main line, the waves catching it and pulling at the rod tip

The truth is that sometimes they can't. The sea is so full of weed that it'll take time to clear. But if the weed is all rafted into one or two masses it will tend to float with the prevailing wind. Thus, if the wind is a north-westerly and the beach runs north to south, in time, most of the weed will end up down at the beach's southern end and the northern end may be fishable. In a straight onshore breeze, the weed may be concentrated in the first thirty yards of surf from the water's edge. Then, wading out a bit and holding the rod upright (long rods give an advantage here) and keeping the line fairly tight to the sinker will avoid the worst of it. Some beaches have lateral currents that are strongest, for example, on the early flood (or at other times of the tide). These will sweep any weed that may be present along with them in a direct collision-course with your line, so when the stuff is about, forego such times and fish over the rest of the tide. Such periods are identifiable by good old trial-and-error and once you have established the pattern of water and weed movement you can pretty much rely on it repeating itself. So, although weed can sometimes wreck prospects, with a bit of thought in many cases it can be outsmarted.

Wash-up zone
With a bit of cunning, weed can be avoided. This accumulation is at the western end of the beach at Pwllheli, after an easterly wind has been blowing for several days

Fished in the right conditions with the right baits, the shallow sandy beaches of Cardigan Bay offer many miles of excellent potential. They even throw up the occasional surprise. Mackerel are common at times in the summer and early autumn months off all types of venues, but one of the most amazing experiences I have ever had whilst fishing was at Borth on a late evening in September 2007. When I arrived, close to low water, I could see clouds of seabirds wheeling in the dusk sky – always a sign of a feeding frenzy in progress. On the beach, there were two guys fishing, the birds diving within their casting range. They'd not had anything all evening, they told me.

I set up a rod, tied on a string of mackerel feathers and first cast had one, then another, and another. They were coming in ones, twos and threes every cast. Then I noticed an even greater commotion a couple of hundred yards to the north along the waterline, where the birds were going absolutely crazy. I headed over there and waded out until I was in about a foot of water, and looked down. I was standing in the middle of many thousands of whitebait and sandeels. They swarmed about me, darting this way and that, so that, at times, patches of the seabed itself seemed to be on the move – then, dark, streamlined predatory shapes swept in, slashing through the shoals, again and again. Whitebait were jumping in dozens out of the water, many beaching themselves in their efforts to escape. Within minutes the sand at the water's edge was a carpet of gleaming silver. Everywhere around me I could see the mackerel as they shot to and fro in their feeding frenzy, passing within inches of me, charging between the boots of my waders, totally oblivious to my presence. At times, I was simply dipping my feathers into the water and catching strings of them, so intent were they on snapping at anything that moved. In no time I had enough fish for food and bait, but the frenzy around me continued without respite until night finally gathered its shadows over sand and surf and all became silent. I have no photographic record of this incident, but it remains so firmly etched on my mind that I can still see it as though it happened five minutes ago – it was an extraordinary thing to have been part of and a great privilege to have witnessed.

Steep shingle beaches

Steep shingle beaches are in some ways a bit trickier to fish than shallow sandy ones, for the simple reason that they don't uncover so much at low tide. Some do strip back to reveal a little sand (which soon covers again on the early flood tide) whilst others just appear to slope on down into the water. Therefore, you cannot easily tell, at a glance, what sort of ground you will be fishing over. It may be clean sand, there may be snags, there may be beds of eelgrass and other weed, it may be flat or it may have interesting gullies and banks.

Rather than just 'chuck-and-see' (which admittedly we all have to do from time to time), a reconnaissance can be a

good idea. Pick a day with a bit of wind so there will be a surf running and head down at low water. This gives you the best chance of spotting any offshore sandbanks. If they reach close enough to the surface, even if some way out, their position will be given away by waves breaking over them in a line. Likewise, if the breakers rolling in all peter out for a few yards but then reform, it's almost certain that they have gone over a deeper gully. An isolated spot that is creating white water is suggestive of the presence of a shallow patch protruding from an otherwise deeper seabed, such as a rocky outcrop or a clump of kelp-covered boulders. Casting your baits either into a gully or just landward of a feature that is causing breakers to form will put it in a spot with improved prospects for success. Another useful thing to figure out is where the sloping shingle meets the flatter seabed. Such a change of angle, running the length of the beach, represents a potent food-holding feature situated at short range and well worth investigating with a second rod.

Storm-beach
A classic steep-to-shingle beach – Tan y Bwlch Beach at Aberystwyth

Examine the strand line to see what's washed up. If there's lots of eelgrass and not much else, then it's likely that, out there, there are eelgrass beds that fish such as black bream often inhabit. Mixed weed will tell you a lot less, as it travels around all over the place. One type dominating suggests a more local origin. Abundant clam and razor shells would suggest the presence of sand and the attendant flatfish. Mussels would suggest the presence of areas of stony ground, the location of which will expand the range of species considerably. Such observations, carefully interpreted, will help you focus your fishing methods to target what is likely to be there.

Because shingle beaches offer access to deeper water, especially at high tide, they are less affected by moderate swells than their shallower counterparts. Just a quick note of caution though, bigger swells can surge up (and down) such beaches with astonishing force. Just go and watch at high tide if a 10ft plus swell is forecast and you'll see what I mean. Only the foolhardy would attempt to fish in such conditions.

The mixture of sand with stony and weedy patches that is often to be found beneath the low water mark along such beaches provides sanctuary to many small fish, such as juvenile flounders, whiting, pouting, blennies, wrasse, gobies and so on. Where small fish congregate one can also expect their predators, such as rays, dogfish and bull huss. Some of these beaches even produce occasional tope in the summer months – Pwllheli being one example. Others, where the ground holds a lot of crabs, can be worth trying with crab baits for smooth-hounds on summer nights. The same tactics can also produce bass. Night fishing in winter will likely produce whiting, pouting and rockling in good numbers, with codling a distinct possibility, especially after a bit of rough weather. Such beaches in fact hold a surprising range of species, which adds to the fun as you don't always know what's coming up next – dragonets, various gurnards or even oddities like red mullet being additional possibilities.

On early morning and late evening high tides, especially in

the summer, active predators will drive baitfish against the shingle, using it to trap them densely, before rushing through and swallowing as many as possible. Lure fishing then comes into its own, with mackerel, garfish and bass all close-in and in feeding mood. Bass will also be caught at such times on large fish baits dropped in at very short range.

Such marks create their own memories. Out of many, I recall one in particular. On a Friday night (just before Christmas 2003), I had abandoned the idea of warm fires, Guinness and cribbage in my local – it being 'Works Friday' the place would have been packed – and instead headed over to Tywyn, arriving just after high tide. Conditions were quite reasonable – an onshore breeze, a good chop but not too much swell. I had the beach to myself, so chose a favourite spot where the shingle ramps down towards flat sand, which is exposed a little at low water. Setting up one rod with a big hook and lugworm/squid bait and another with a two hook rig with smaller hooks and baits, I fished down the ebb in darkness. To the small baits there came a succession of whiting and dabs with the occasional pouting, but there was no interest in the large bait.

It got to the time when I was starting to think that a couple of pints was not such a bad idea after all, when the rod with the two-hook rig registered a savage, lunging bite. This was no whiting. I grabbed the rod and a heavy tussle resulted. This carried on until the fish reached the breakers where it let go and the line immediately went slack. I carried on reeling in – something was there but nothing like the weight of before. A sorry sight greeted me – a five-bearded rockling, lifeless and scored deeply down either side, with its fins badly shredded. It had quietly taken the bait and something must then have grabbed it, but the small hook had not made contact with the larger fish.

Postponing the pub, I reeled in the lugworm/squid bait, which was ready to be changed in any case. Rebaiting the rig with the mangled rockling, I cast it out as far as I could. And waited. And waited. Luckily the whiting and dabs were biting again, so the occasional fish was coming in on the two hook rod. In the end, I decided it was packing-up time. I brought in the two-hooker, stripped off the remains of the bait and cut off the rig. Wiping my hands with a cloth, I turned and instantly noticed the other rod nodding and bending furiously. This time I picked up the rod, waited a moment for a heavy pull and struck hard. Again that heavy weight, and once it was in the surf it bored off down-tide, bending the rod hard over, so that I had to run towards the sea to give it line. I managed to turn it and all of a sudden it was through the breakers and beached – a cod that sent my scales to 6.5lb. It was a magnificent sight and a personal best on Cardigan Bay shore, a coastline not noted for big cod. By directly observing what the cod were feeding on (smaller members of their own family) and following through by putting that knowledge into practice, I had scored – where textbook baits had not. And there was still time to grab a pint at last orders.

Mixed ground

Mixed ground, whether deep or shallow (and it is often shallow) typically consists of vast expanses featuring numerous bouldery, weed-covered mounds that are interspersed with patches of sand. In some areas, the sand to boulders ratio may be around fifty-fifty: in others it's boulders all the way. With the wrong approach, such areas are difficult to fish, costly on tackle and leading to frustration and frayed tempers.

These apparently poor odds can, however, be strongly improved in your favour. The advent of online satellite and aerial photography has made detailed reconnaissance of such venues, including the all-important sub-tidal zone below the low water mark, possible from the comfort of home. Locate the venue that you want to investigate and zoom in. Sub-tidal sand-patches, showing up pale against the contrasting dark background of boulders and weed, are what you need to look for and the scale-bar will indicate their size. An area of sand, some 20 by 20 yards in size and surrounded by food-rich rough ground, is an ideal target. Make sure that you can identify it, once at the venue, from landmarks such as other sand-patches or distinctive rocky features, that are situated above the low water mark. Once a likely spot has been picked, print out the image, get it laminated to make it waterproof and take it with you to the venue. This will be a daytime visit, set to coincide with low water on a spring tide in order to confidently locate the feature on the ground. Fish it using an accurately-cast scent-rich bait, like a fillet of mackerel, large sandeel or soft crab and any fish foraging amongst the nearby rocks and weed will pick up the scent trail and be prompted to investigate.

Mixed ground is big fish country, so use big baits. Small baits will be ripped to bits by mini-species like corkwing wrasse and blennies and the ever-present legions of crabs. Think big and you may get a nice surprise – bass, smooth-hound,

Rough country
A typical mixed-ground beach at Tonfanau, near Tywyn; rich in food but difficult to fish

bull huss and in autumn and winter codling are all on the list of possibilities. Sometimes though, swarms of dogfish will dominate things, but that's true of almost all venues.

Even on the clean sand areas, there will be isolated weedy rocks. Here's where you can do yourself another favour – always fish just one hook. It is no fun to have a tremendous bite and be reeling in a good fish, only for the other hook to snag into something. Don't even give it a chance of happening. A running leger-rig means that when retrieving a fish your sinker isn't going to drag through the graunch and get stuck. When you need to change bait, strike and retrieve like mad, bringing in your rig high in the water above the snags. Another tactic that further improves the odds is to use a 'rotten bottom' rig, in which the metal attachment loop that sticks out of the top of the sinker is hung from an open hook-shaped clip for the cast, the connecting line between the loop and clip being light 10 to 15lb mono – the idea is that when the rig hits the sea surface the lead jumps off the clip. If for any reason the lead gets stuck and you have a fish on, the weak line connecting the lead to the rig will break allowing you to land the fish. A lost lead will react with the sea water, quickly developing a white coating of rather insoluble lead chloride, which stops it from further dissolving away – and in any case you can always go back at low tide the next day and see if you can find it again!

The best sea conditions at mixed ground venues are gentle onshore chops, creating enough movement in the water but not pushing your main line about too much. In contrast, a hard surf will see your main line get mixed up with any fronds of weed it comes close to, the resultant tangles decreasing your chances of retrieving your rig. Floating weed is an occupational hazard of such places but in my experience the weed is often only close in. In such cases, carefully wade out past as much of the stuff as possible, cast and fish holding your rod. You should then be clear of the worst of it.

One June evening in 2011 a regular fishing buddy and I trudged across many acres of slippery boulders to fish such a sand patch. The quarry was tope – not because we were expecting them but to see if they were possible from the venue in question, as kayak anglers had recently caught a few close inshore in this area. Having cheerfully noted the lack of floating weed, we both rigged up with running legers baited with mackerel fillets and, casting a moderate distance, dropped them onto the sand in a few feet of water, put the reels on ratchet and sat back enjoying the view. After a while, my mate reeled in a dogfish, and shortly afterwards my rod tip began to nod in that insistent way that would normally indicate that another doggie had found my bait.

Lazily picking up the rod and striking (as one does when one's lifetime dogfish tally runs into the thousands), I was surprised to be met with the distinctive, 'backing-off' resistance, suggesting the presence of a bull huss, another regular catch at the mark. It backed off, I countered, and next thing the fish, no longer a huss either, set off at a blistering run, tearing off leftwards and downtide towards my mate. I hollered over to him, 'I say, what on earth is this?' (or words to that effect). Was it perhaps our target species? If so, it was heavy yet not huge, so applying maximum pressure I turned it towards me and suddenly it was splashing and thrashing in the surf, unable to gain purchase in the shallow water. The identity was now quite clear. It was a beautiful bass of just over 30 inches in length with an estimated weight of 10.5 to 11.5lbs (according to the measurement/weight formula devised by the Bass Anglers Sportfishing Society). It had seriously beaten my personal best for the species and it was my first 'double figure' specimen. A prime spawning fish, likely over 20 years old, she was quickly photographed before I carried her into knee-deep water, holding her upright. In a few seconds, she recovered her composure and shot off seawards with a couple of swishes of her great, paddle-like tail. I like eating bass, but such individuals are our prime spawning stock, the very foundation of the species and its viability. 'Go away and make more four-pounders', was my parting shot.

Shallow reefs

The extensive shallow reefs that are such a feature of the coast both north and south of Aberystwyth offer a splendid challenge to the dedicated anglers that regularly fish them. Bass are their quarry, but they will all have accounts of other decent fish that they have encountered over the years, from codling to conger eels.

Nature's larder
Shallow, gullied reefs are food-rich areas that are well worth fishing, with their margins and gully mouths both top areas to try

Along these sections of the coast, wave action over many centuries has eroded away the crumbly cliffs, which have slowly retreated landwards, leaving behind acres of flattish rock, worn down to around the high water wave-base. Deeply gullied in places, especially around the reef margins where bands of softer rock have been carved out, pockmarked with rock-pools large and small and having all sorts of nooks and crannies, shallow reefs are teeming with life.

In terms of their marine biology, such reefs are very clearly zoned. Below the bases of the cliffs there is naked rock, often covered in fallen debris from above and reminding the angler not to walk right under the tottering rock faces of shale and grit. This barren-looking zone gives way seaward to green weed-covered smooth rock (lethally slippery), before the zone in which the barnacles dwell is reached. Reassuringly rough underfoot, away from patches of bladderwrack, barnacled rock with its frequent patches of small mussels forms the most extensive zone on most of these reefs. In settled conditions, the rock pools are alive with prawns, crabs and small fish like blennies. Once, whilst collecting prawns for bait, I poked a stick into a deep crevice under an overhang and a good-sized lobster came trotting out into my net.

The barnacle zone finally gives way to kelp-draped rock which is only visible at low water on spring tides as a rule. Beyond the water's edge, fingers of rock jut out, giving way to mixed ground or in places, clean sand. Often, the sand is flat lying and constitutes something of a marine desert, but locally, where reefs stick out into the current, the scouring force of the tide has formed systems of sandbanks and gullies. These can often only be found via trial and error.

Fish will be where the food is, and at such venues, unless there is a permanently underwater offshore reef within casting range, that means fishing close to the rocks which is why one often sees anglers float fishing or spinning around the mouths of the gullies. Float fishing is a pleasant enough way to catch bass. However, it demands co-operative weather. A strong wind will take your float from just where you want it at the mouth of a gully straight into the weedy rocks to one side or the other resulting in snagging. A big swell will have a similar effect, and a really big swell could knock you into the water – so keep away at such times. These marks are best explored under relatively benign conditions.

The gullies that split these shallow reefs are themselves shallow too, so that a sliding float fixed to fish at 3 to 4ft down will do the job in most situations. In terms of bait, peeler or soft crab reigns supreme during spring and early summer,

Reef at Borth
The shallow reef at Borth on a low spring tide, with the kelp zone exposed around the gully-entrances

when the fish are actively and often exclusively seeking it. Prawns, either fished alone or in combination with crab, are also very effective during the summer months. The target is bass, although occasional codling and ballan wrasse are both possible, as are dogfish. In high summer (when all the predator species are busy eating one another), lures are effective, and mackerel and garfish can be added to the list, together with not infrequent gurnards and occasional greater weevers at longer range over the sand. In autumn and winter, storms often render such places inaccessible. In calmer conditions, clean sand at range produces winter dabs, pouting and whiting - but that goes for most venues, including many easier to reach!

Dogfish are abundant in Cardigan Bay, and no more so than in rocky areas such as these. Night fishing with leger tackle and fish baits will yield one after another in grim monotony, occasionally interrupted by a conger or a bull huss. Other species that might turn up include spotted ray and three-bearded rockling, these more so in the winter and early spring months.

That fish move in on the flood tide to see what food there is should come as no surprise to any experienced angler, but it's still surprising how acute this switch can be. I learned that in a very effective manner over 25 years ago when one evening a regular fishing buddy and I walked out on the last of the ebb to the edge of the reef at the south end of Tan-y-Bwlch Beach near Aberystwyth. Slippery and weed-covered, it was awkward to approach but it looked as fishy as any other reef of this nature, with an abundance of food. On this evening, my mate and I sneaked up to the water's edge, deliberately keeping a low profile, and as the flood started, flicked crab baits just ten yards out. We both had bites within seconds – mine was a big rockling whilst his was a nice bass of 4lb. This was a remarkable demonstration of how close to the water's edge some fish will hunt.

Deep water rock marks

From Newquay down to St David's Head and around the south-west of the Llŷn Peninsula are a host of marks that produce superb fishing, but which also demand the utmost respect. In this instance, a safety briefing is warranted first and foremost. Fishing almost anywhere in bad weather tends to vary between being uncomfortable and a complete waste of time. On deep water rock marks, it could easily cost you your life. There are three critical factors to take into account:

Firstly, rain. What feels good and rough underfoot when dry can turn into a non-stick skidpan following just a shower. These are not good places to slip at the best of times and should be avoided if rain is forecast in any shape or form. Secondly, wind. Anything vaguely onshore of force 4 and above will bring rough seas crashing in. Thirdly, swell. Even if winds are light, a heavy swell can produce seriously large waves. I hope I'm being clear here. Any conditions that could lead to you ending up in the water should be strictly avoided. I guess alcohol could sensibly be added to the list of things to avoid, too. Some of the rocky headlands along the coast create their own tidal rips due to the constriction they present to the tidal flow. These can bomb along past the rocks at several knots. Fall into a riptide and you could be carried beyond help in no time, in a remote area that will almost invariably have no mobile phone reception. Fishing with a companion who can raise the alarm and wearing a life jacket or in winter a flotation suit, will give you a chance of survival should you fall in, but it is best not to tempt providence in the first place!

So let us assume that you are physically fit, the weather is fine and settled, it has not rained in the past 24 hours and a light breeze and just a foot of swell is lapping at the rocks down at the water's edge. What are the possibilities? Very many!

Deep water rock marks allow access to a whole variety of types of ground, from the most hideously snaggy to squeaky clean, in 30ft to over 100ft of water. They offer the chance to explore miles of spectacular coastal scenery on a fine day. Indeed, an initial reconnaissance, unencumbered by fishing gear, makes for a grand day out in its own right. During its course, you can identify likely ledges, assess the feasibility of getting down to them with all your gear (which will critically depend on your fitness, ability to move across rocky terrain and so on) and observe how waves, swells and tides affect the area to be fished. Approaches to rock marks present a whole spectrum of difficulty. Some require nothing more than an easy scramble whilst at the other end of the scale there are steep and exposed descents, requiring the use of climbing ropes, hardware and knowledge of belaying techniques. Unless you are already a rock-climber, start with the easy ones. Do not take a seat-box with you – it will make movement across steep rock awkward (if not downright dangerous) as it can throw you off balance. Stow all your bits and pieces in suitable containers and put them in a climber's rucksack. This will make for much easier and safer progress.

Rocky seabeds giving way within 20-30 yards to clean sand are fairly typical of the deep water rock marks along the Ceredigion coast between Newquay and Cardigan, but sandy patches can also be found with patience in the rougher areas of Pembroke and the Llŷn. These are fished for a range of species using baits presented hard on the seabed, from flatfish

Rock fishing
Deep water rock marks can offer peaceful fishing – if and only if the weather is settled

A time to be cautious
In heavy seas such as these at Strumble Head during a winter gale, the dangers of venturing onto rock marks are self-evident

Not for the unwary
A good head for heights is needed when approaching many deep water rock marks and a reconnaissance unencumbered by fishing gear is recommended

like plaice, small predators like gurnards and dogfish up to the bigger predators like rays, huss or even tope. Landing a big tope from such a spot is a serious business – not something I'd want to try without a couple of experienced mates around. Other people prefer to stick to mackerel bashing or, in autumn, pulling up strings of whiting, pouting and dabs.

Where tidal rips occur, it is often the case that holding ground is easier at certain stages of the tide and harder at others. One mark I know well (one of the ledges at Mwnt, near Cardigan) has just a gentle push of water on the ebb, but when the flood bombs past, it can drag a rig anchored by a grip lead into the snags that are off to one side. During reconnaissance trips, such rips can often be identified by areas of disturbed water which look like the rapids on a river – in extreme cases having one large standing wave after another. Where larger positive undersea features (like pinnacles) are present, you may see smooth, glassy areas on the sea surface, where the water is upwelling as it is forced up and over restrictions. Whirlpools occur locally and are often marked as hazards on Admiralty charts for mariners. Such charts are therefore well worth checking as part of your research. As to the timing of riptides, remember that in Cardigan Bay, the general tidal flow runs up around the coast from south to north on the flood and the opposite way on the ebb. Rips occur at the point of (and extend down tide of) a headland, so on an ebb tide look for disturbed water towards the south, on a flood tide towards the north.

The tumult that is going on underwater where a riptide is at work, sweeping hapless baitfish along to where the predators are waiting, is the reason why they are of interest to the angler. To me, the best fishing from deep water rock marks is that which dispenses with bait completely. The trick is to carefully seek out safe positions within casting range of riptides and fish them with lures. These are the waters that small pirks, artificial sandeels, shads and the like were designed for. The target is primarily pollack, but mackerel and at times coalfish, bass or codling will also frequent such areas. A day spent walking to and from such a mark, the climbing to access the fishing position, fishing it intensively for a few hours and the

Riptide!
One of the many tidal rips that occur around Bardsey Sound at various stages of the tide, discernable by the disturbed water and smooth areas marking upwelling

climb back out is an excellent way to keep fit. Casting lures 80 yards out into a riptide time and again and retrieving through this deep, fast moving water is certainly strenuous exercise, but the effort can be rewarded by good bags of fish and some fine specimens, too.

Where rocky coastlines are incised by deep, sheltered inlets, the tidal flow is often a lot less, especially during the hours around slack water, enabling the more relaxing pursuit of bait fishing. Such places are the haunts of a wide range of species – members of the wrasse family, rocklings, conger eels, bull huss, dogfish, pollack, pouting, poor cod, codling, occasional ling and the mini-species. Set back a little from the open sea, inlets are a little less exposed to waves and swell, though the same safety rules should at all times be applied. Single hook rigs fished from a strong main line are usual, and a 'rotten bottom system' can again improve your odds. But shop-bought leads are expensive if you are losing one every cast and all sorts of things can been used as substitutes: wheel nuts, pebbles with holes through them, old spark plugs and so on. Shape is of no importance where casting distance is not an issue.

If you do get snagged, you will need to pull until the hook straightens or the line breaks. Do not lose your temper and start striking hard with the rod. It will rarely help at all and it is an easy way to break a rod. Instead, shrug your shoulders, put the reel into free spool, put the rod down somewhere safe then pull the line up hand-over-hand until tight. Next, wind the tightened line onto an appropriate handle. I use my fish clonker for the job. Wind the line on for several turns until it won't slip, steady your footing and pull, gripping the handle with both hands, until your rig comes free or the line breaks. Next cast, avoid that spot as you now know it is especially snaggy.

During my 2009 'species hunt' (when I successfully set out to catch forty fish species from the Welsh shore in a year), I was always aware that a conger would be required. They are common along the rockier areas of the Cardigan Bay coast and should therefore represent a relatively easy addition to the tally. So I started late in the year for this species and was full of anticipation when I arrived at Mwnt late one mid-October afternoon – success would make it species #38 for the year.

It was a clear evening. The climb down to the fishing ledge I had chosen is easy but steep. From above it looks like you need ropes to climb down it, but in reality there are large positive handholds everywhere once you are on it, so many in fact that an octopus would be spoiled for choice. Halfway down, the old rucksack in which all my gear was stashed decided to part company with my back as one, then both straps, disintegrated. Gear tipped out, bounced down and spilled all over the place. (Mental note registered – things wear out and when they do, replace them!)

I gathered everything together again and set up with both rods fishing close-in: one for any odd species that might turn up, the other for conger-baits like pouting, while daylight lasted. I was setting up the second rod when the first attempted to take off seaward. A good-sized ballan wrasse was the culprit. That set the scene for the next hour, with wrasse, pollack, dogfish, poor cod and pouting trickling in. An exceptional sunset over Cardigan Island followed so I stopped fishing for a while and alternately concentrated on photography and on simply being there, alone on my rock-perch above the shadowy deeps and beneath the incandescent heavens.

Night fell, so it was on with the head torch and out over the side with the conger rig which consisted of a heavy hook-length, big hook and large pouting fillet. Almost every textbook recommends such tactics (because they work) and I knew that conger were resident there so the chances of success seemed at least reasonable. The other rod I dropped close-in too, armed with a small size 4 ragworm-baited hook, more out of curiosity than anything. Repeated tweaks on the big fish rig led to one bent hook or break-off after another – I began to suspect small fish, lobsters and crabs were nudging the bait about until everything got well and truly stuck. Then a small bite registered on the ragworm-baited rod. I grabbed it and, at a better pull, struck into a surprisingly heavy weight. A conger in the 6 to 8lb range slowly came into view, surfaced, was very, very carefully lifted the ten feet up from the sea, photographed, unhooked from the small hook and quickly returned. Species number 38 was in the bag! Temperatures were now dropping fast beneath clear skies and dew was forming all over the rocks. I could feel the change underfoot and cleared out fairly soon afterwards, the climb back up with my temporarily repaired rucksack requiring serious concentration to avoid slipping. But the trip had achieved its objective and once again I was reminded that it is anglers and not fish that study textbooks. It is hoped, however, that this book will encourage the open-minded approach!

Estuaries

The estuaries of the main rivers draining the Welsh mountains form wide, expansive wildernesses at low tide, with flats of sand and mud here, shifting sandbars there and braided channels dissecting both as they wind their way down towards the open sea. Inland, the channels may be rather inaccessible without a serious trek, but nearer to where they flow out into the sea access is far easier – in most cases such spots are also home to a fishing harbour. The ground varies – outer parts of estuaries typically consist of sand with patches of mixed ground colonised by weed beds. Further inland, the sand gradually gives way to mud. Soft mud or loose waterlogged sand presents an obvious hazard, so when investigating potential marks to fish, take a good walking stick with you and probe any dodgy-looking areas before deciding whether to cross them. In particular, keep off sandbars that clearly get cut-off and then covered by the tide – getting stuck is bad enough in its own right, but with the tide flooding in quickly, as it often does in estuaries, the situation could rapidly deteriorate from an inconvenience to an emergency. If planning a night fishing trip, a reconnaissance during daylight is essential.

Estuaries are teeming with biodiversity because of the great variety of ecosystems that they contain: channels, rocks, weed beds, sandbars, mudflats and salt marshes that are variably covered twice a day by saline or brackish waters. With this abundance and variety of life, it is no wonder that fish are attracted to estuaries in large numbers. All estuaries have their resident fish populations plus seasonal visitors. Thus, brackish water dwellers like flounders, eels and mullet are there pretty much most of the time. Bass are also resident for most of the year. In summer, plaice, turbot, garfish, small pollack, lesser weevers and sand smelts take up residence

Channels and bars
Weed-fringed channels, teeming with life, alternate with sandbars in the Dyfi Estuary. A low tide reconnaissance in daylight always pays off

An expansive
wilderness
*The outer reaches
of estuaries often
present a maze of
sandbars and
gullies at low tide.
This is the outfall of
the Dyfi Estuary*

and mackerel may visit on the larger tides in the outer reaches. In autumn, whiting, dabs, codling and dogfish are all possible. So variety is on the cards at most times of year. The one time when estuaries are best avoided is after prolonged heavy rain fills them with fresh water – the fish then mostly move out into the open sea until salinity levels have been restored.

Estuaries offer an escape route when the weather is too rough or the swell too large to fish the local beaches and they can often fish better when there's a bit of a chop on the water. The important consideration is tides. In many estuaries, the full tidal flow, especially on spring tides, is too strong for the angler to hold ground. This is not down to insufficient lead weight, but weed. There are few occasions when the water in estuaries is weed free – it grows along the intertidal fringes in extensive beds, where bits get broken off by people searching for crabs. Many estuaries are used extensively for motorised water sports and the wakes from powerboats do their fair share of weed liberation, too. Still more weed gets carried in on the tide from the adjacent open sea after gales. When the tide is running hard it only takes a few handfuls of it around your line and you will have a really difficult job hauling it back in against the pressure of the current. So lesson one is to avoid times of faster tidal flow. The middle two hours of the flood and ebb are peak flow times. Concentrate over low and high water instead.

Low tides offer the chance to fish the last two or three hours of the ebb, which can be productive for flatfish, and the first two or three hours of the flood. From spring through to autumn, each new flood-tide brings with it bass, which run up the estuary with the current, feeding as they go. Slack low water coinciding with first light is a good time to spin for the bass as they group up at estuary mouths, ready to run with the new tide. In summer, garfish are often taken on spinners too. With respect to bait fishing and weed, the best advice is to keep fishing until the weed starts to become a problem – after that it will only get worse, so pack up before it becomes horrendous!

High water on big spring tides will fill estuaries literally to the brim, covering the acres of flats that lie alongside the channels. This makes many marks inaccessible, but given that bass run with the tide, the couple of hours before high water in an estuary's upper reaches might produce a fish or two, and flounders are commonly caught where fresh and saltwater meet. In the case of the smaller neap tides there is better news. Neaps may not overtop the channel sides, so that you can fish the channels over high tide at many spots. This will give you a window of opportunity the duration of which will be dictated by the weed situation – it may be as long as two hours, or it may only cover the slack water period.

The best estuary fishing in my experience is for flounders and dabs from autumn through to New Year, for bass in spring to early summer and for mixed bags on high water neaps in autumn. During the holiday season, and at weekends, the water is often taken over completely by jetskis and other noisy

The competition
*Estuaries offer good
fishing, but turn up
before other visitors
have arrived or after
they have gone
home*

monstrosities, although fishing at night and in the very early morning is still feasible.

With respect to baits, there is one factor to take into account at estuary venues, more so than elsewhere, and that is the countless crabs that live amongst the weed beds or buried in the sand. Small armies of them stalk hungrily across the seabed, stripping any baited hooks they come across in minutes. To give the fish a chance of finding your offering, stick to tough baits such as black lugworms or salted razor. Peeler or soft crab, lashed to the hook with bait-elastic, is even better as although crabs can at times be cannibalistic, they don't seem quite so keen to tuck into one of their own, especially if the next angler along from you is feeding them with prime fresh ragworm. Leger rigs keep such baits where the fish expect to find them – on the bottom. At the height of summer, float fishing with sandeels for bass or with thin strips of mackerel for garfish can be worthwhile, although with strong currents and floating weed it can be difficult outside of the slack water periods. Last but not least, for the specialist there is mullet fishing, which will be discussed in the section on fish species.

One of the biggest surprises I have had in my entire shore angling career came within the first few weeks of starting out. My kit was somewhat rudimentary at the time. I had one outfit, consisting of a 7ft hollow glass fibre boat rod and a second-hand multiplier reel that I was struggling to get the hang of. The contrast with today could hardly be greater. There were no internet forums, very limited choice in tackle and bait for a skint twenty-year-old, and despite there being such a variety of fishing grounds close to hand, I frankly didn't have a clue. I had yet to catch anything at all.

It was a bleak, winter-grey February afternoon and I had read in one of the fishing magazines that the Leri estuary was a good place for winter flounders on fish baits so I bought a herring from a fishmonger in Aberystwyth and headed down there. With size 1 'bait-holder' hooks (the only ones I had) I put together what looked vaguely like a rig, baited it with thin slivers of herring and began casting out into the middle of the narrow muddy channel, sometimes successfully. After a couple of hours I was starting to wonder if I should believe what I read in the magazines – not even the crabs seemed interested. Just then, the rod slammed over as if a low-flying gull had collided with the line. I grabbed it, felt the weight of a sizeable fish thrashing about, started reeling in and with a couple of good shakes of its head, off it came. Quickly baiting up again I cast out to the same spot, thankfully without a bird's nest, and sat holding the rod. Within moments, it arched over solidly again and this time I struck back hard. After a heavy tussle the catch came into view, no flounder this, but a sea-trout of around 5lbs! That was the point at which I realised that yes, I could catch fish, (even if I wasn't allowed to keep this one). It was an amazing moment. Within weeks I was better kitted-out and had started fishing in earnest, learning how to hunt the spring bass over the reefs. That first boost in self-confidence though was something I will never forget.

Man-made structures

The breakwaters constructed to protect our main harbours offer congenial fishing and are often places where locals meet up on a summer's evening for a bit of fishing and a lot of gossip. They are pleasant enough places to fish from. Crowded on occasion, when the mackerel are in and everyone's after a few, at other times there's almost always room to fish. Typically, a breakwater has very rough ground close-in with mixed or clean ground being found 30 to 50 yards out, beyond the piled, weed-covered boulders that make up its outer defences. Thus, options are quite varied.

The seabed at longer range will carry the range of fish species expected from either clean or mixed ground. Closer in, there will often be many small fish such as shannies and sea scorpions inhabiting the gaps between the boulders, various wrasse, rocklings, gobies, pouting and so on. Where larger holes and fissures occur, conger eels will likely be lurking – the challenge is extracting them from such lairs. Dogfish and bull huss inhabit this rough ground too. Bass and pollack, mackerel and garfish hunt along breakwaters where they trap baitfish against the structure and can be hooked on spinners or float-fished sandeels, prawns and fish strips. Most of the smaller species are caught fishing in amongst the rough ground, using small ragworm baits.

Breakwaters are fair weather venues. When the sea's rough, the resident fish hunker down under the boulders, out of the way. In addition, large waves in rough weather can break right over the structure. Anyone caught in such a situation would be washed away together with all their gear. Pick a pleasant day without a swell running and fish up to and over high tide. For congers and the three species of rocklings, night tides are best. Unless you are fishing over the cleaner ground, casting distance is unimportant. Most fish are caught straight down the side – where the risk of snagging is at its least as the angle of your line is good and steep and you have less snags to retrieve your rig over. The comments in the section on deep water rock marks regarding sinkers and getting unstuck also apply here.

Landing a big fish from a breakwater can be tricky when it's a long way down to the water. A weighted 'drop net' on a length of rope can be used, but it requires practice to learn how to control it. If the breakwater adjoins a beach, an alternative tactic involves guiding the fish back along the length of the breakwater to land it on the sand or shingle. This is easier when you have the place to yourself: complications often arise if you have to pass over and under the rods and lines of other

Social sea-angling
Locals and visitors alike enjoy a congenial evening's mackerel fishing at Aberystwyth's Stone Jetty

anglers. It certainly adds to the entertainment though, and a crowd of spectators can be expected to gather, offering all sorts of advice! Very large breakwaters, such as the big one at Fishguard, have one or more slipways down into the water and when I have fished there in the distant past for conger eels I have always set up on a slipway for ease of landing the catch. If targeting large fish, it is best, when picking your spot, to always first consider how you would land a good-sized specimen from there before committing yourself to fishing it. This beats setting up willy-nilly and then, with a decent fish on, suddenly wondering how the hell you are going to land it!

I well recall one mid-1980s November night at Fishguard. Back then, you could turn up, have a quick word with the watchman and then drive out onto the breakwater. These days, things are far more formal. Anyway, I'd spent the day at the Mwnt rock ledges near Cardigan but the whiting fishing had been slow, so once the flood tide began I thought I'd grab a bite and then push on down to Fishguard. By the time I'd set up it was a dark, starry night, with the inky water slop-slapping against the weed-covered boulders. It's a peaceful, relaxing sound once you get used to it. Odd whiting and pouting were attacking my mackerel baits but it was hardly hectic. Then there was a better bite and I struck into a heavier fish which backed-off a fair bit but in a while I was winning, slowly. In it gradually came, almost within reach now, when everything went solid. The lower hook of the two-hook rig I was using had caught up in the weed at the base of the slipway, with the fish splashing about on the surface. I didn't have a very good headlamp back then so I walked down to see what I'd got. As the fish came within range of the lamp, two luminous green eyes stared back at me, stopping me in my tracks for a moment. I'd been fishing only a few years back then. However, the apprehension that comes from inexperience quickly overcome, I pulled the rig clear of the snag and landed the fish – it was my first (and last) spurdog from the Cardigan Bay shore, a nice fish of around

5lbs. Though, in subsequent years, I and others caught many on long range charter boat trips from Aberystwyth, heading out 20 miles or more in late November, the species was shortly to be all but eliminated from the Bay by commercial longliners. But I can still see those green eyes staring back at me as though it happened yesterday.

A Fishing Tour
around Cardigan Bay

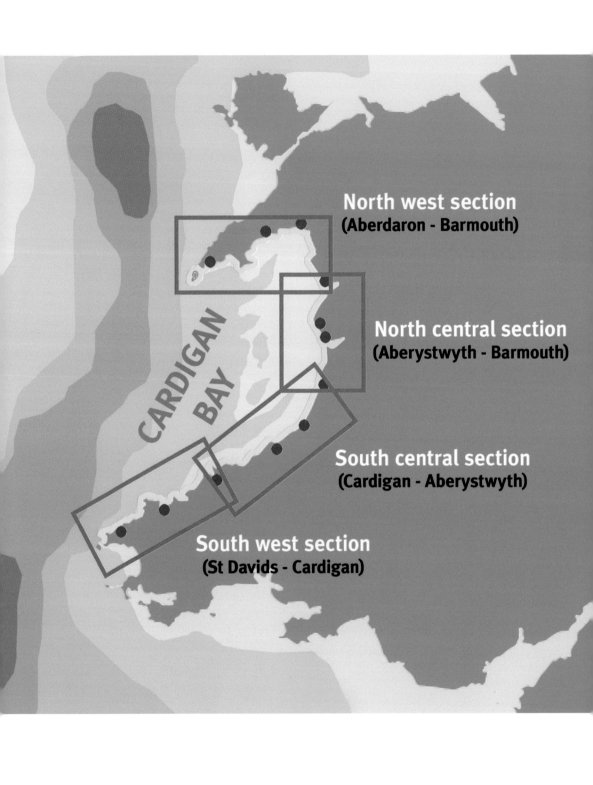

North west section
(Aberdaron - Barmouth)

North central section
(Aberystwyth - Barmouth)

CARDIGAN BAY

South central section
(Cardigan - Aberystwyth)

South west section
(St Davids - Cardigan)

Basic layout of the bay (south to north)

The Cardigan Bay coast is well served by the road network and in addition, many important coastal towns in the northern half are well-connected by rail. The main A487 runs close to the coast all the way from St David's, down in the far south-west, up through Fishguard, Cardigan, Aberaeron and Aberystwyth before turning inland to get around the Dyfi Estuary. From the Dyfi Bridge at Machynlleth, the A493 heads back out to the coast at Aberdyfi and again skirts the coast past Tywyn and Fairbourne, before going inland to bypass the Mawddach Estuary via Dolgellau.

Continuing our whistle stop tour, the A496 then heads out westwards to the coast at Barmouth (Abermaw), before turning north past Llanbedr and Harlech. A final diversion inland around the Glaslyn Estuary leads back to the A487, which is rejoined on its way towards Porthmadog. From Porthmadog the Cardigan Bay coast stretches away westwards and is followed by the A497 through Criccieth and Pwllheli, from where the A499 leads on to Abersoch. Narrower B-roads then wind their way on down to the remote tip of the Llŷn Peninsula at Aberdaron.

These key coastal settlements (and many smaller ones in between) are served by well-signposted minor roads and offer a wide choice of angling venues – some easy to access, some requiring a bit of effort and a few involving a serious physical challenge. In other words, there is something for everyone.

Let's now take a closer look, with some recommended marks – although there are dozens more for those who have some experience, are equipped with 1:25,000 Ordnance

Survey maps and who like to explore. These are just a few for starters. The accompanying maps grade the marks as easy, moderate and hard-core. These are to help anglers select them according to to their own mobility, fitness, climbing ability and so on. Easy marks are where access involves little or no walking and are mostly on level ground (some beaches have a shingle slope at their heads). Moderate marks involve some walking along sand, paths, across shallow rocky reefs and boulder-strewn areas. Hard-core marks involve long walks and/or steep scrambles or climbs, with considerable exposure in places, and are not for beginners unless they can handle heights and are accompanied by somebody with experience of such country.

The north Pembrokeshire coast
Rock-bound all the way with demanding approaches to many marks, but in settled weather the fishing can be rewarding

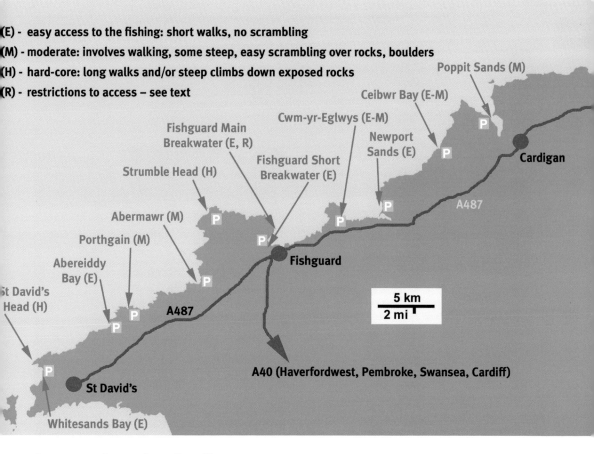

(E) - easy access to the fishing: short walks, no scrambling
(M) - moderate: involves walking, some steep, easy scrambling over rocks, boulders
(H) - hard-core: long walks and/or steep climbs down exposed rocks
(R) - restrictions to access – see text

Poppit Sands (M)

Ceibwr Bay (E-M)

Cwm-yr-Eglwys (E-M)

Fishguard Main
Breakwater (E, R)

Newport
Sands (E)

Cardigan

Fishguard Short
Breakwater (E)

Strumble Head (H)

A487

Abermawr (M)

Porthgain (M)

Fishguard

Abereiddy
Bay (E)

St David's
Head (H)

5 km
2 mi

A487

A40 (Haverfordwest, Pembroke, Swansea, Cardiff)

St David's

Whitesands Bay (E)

Ramsey Sound to Cardigan
(the south-west section)

Predominantly craggy, this section of the Cardigan Bay coast still offers a number of more accessible and user-friendly venues dotted along its length. For the serious rock angler however, with bags of stamina, good settled weather and the time to explore, it offers almost unlimited potential.

We begin with the northern end of the tide-ripped and notorious Ramsey Sound. This area is reached by following the minor roads westward from St David's to St Justinian's, home of the local Lifeboat and where limited parking is possible (more so out of peak holiday season). Here, one can take the Coastal Path northwards and wander past dozens of rock platforms. Those around Point St John, looking out towards the offshore rocks of Carreg-gafeiliog, are particularly popular

Ramsey Sound
*Swirling, reef-ridden
waters. Point St John
is the headland on
the left*

when suitable conditions prevail. Throughout this area the fishing is for pollack and mackerel using lures; wrasse on float-fished or legered crab and worm baits; and huss or conger on heavy leger gear.

Around the corner is the idyllic, west-facing sweep of sand and surf of Whitesands Bay – an extremely popular beach with the water sports fraternity. Reached by another signposted minor road from St David's, it has a large car park to cater for its myriad visitors. When a surf is running in a westerly breeze, it can be fished for bass and flatfish – mostly flounders and dabs with the chance of a turbot or plaice. Winter brings more dabs plus whiting, dogfish and a few coalfish. Because of its popularity, this is a venue best visited by night and early in the morning, when the surfers are not massing in the waves.

St David's Head, a long and craggy headland deeply incised on its northern side by a large inlet, is a half-hour tramp along the Coastal Path northwards from the car park at Whitesands Bay. Once out on the headland there are a

Whitesands Bay
Cardigan Bay's first big surf beach going north. Fish it by night to avoid potential conflicts of interest

number of rock platforms accessible by careful scrambling. A degree of competence on steep rock and a head for heights are required to reach many spots. Like all rock marks, these are fair weather venues requiring light winds, a light swell and dry, settled conditions to fish in safety. If, from the car park at Whitesands Bay, the surfing conditions look impressive, then the swell is almost certainly going to be hazardous out on the rocks. Take care. Serious fishing is sometimes practised

St David's Head
Strictly a fair-weather venue

Evening at Abereiddy Bay, sandy bottomed and rock-fringed

here, when conditions are safe, for huss and conger. A more leisurely pastime involves the good wrasse fishing on sunny summer afternoons and sometimes excellent lure fishing for quality pollack, mackerel and coalfish.

North-east from St David's Head the coast, for the half dozen miles up to Abereiddy Bay, is impressively cliff-bound. The fact that some sections are popular with rock climbers hints to the caution that should be exercised by the average pedestrian.

The broad, west facing sweep of Abereiddy Bay offers easy vehicle access and a sandy beach interspersed at its south-west end with fingers of rock. More sand is accessible over the low water period. The beach can take on a good surf when the wind is in the west, with bass, flatfish and dogfish all likely catches. Rockier country producing huss, conger, pollack, wrasse, mackerel and other species is encountered to either side of the bay. Even if scrambling down to the rock ledges does not appeal to you, a short walk along the coastal path to the north of the bay is worthwhile just to look upon the famous Blue Hole. This was a deep slate quarry that the sea has broken into – a remarkable sight.

Porthgain
*Porthgain harbour
entrance. The coast
hereabouts has an
abundance of rock
ledges to fish when
conditions are settled*

The next road access point to the north-east is at the picturesque fishing village of Porthgain, with its impressive array of old lime kilns. At the time that these were in use, road transport of bulk materials was difficult and it was easier to bring the limestone and coal in by boat, make the lime at the landing point and then distribute it inland for building or agricultural purposes. Around the harbour and along the coast path on either side there are plenty of rock ledges available to the agile, producing a similar range of species to the rocks around Abereiddy and St David's Head.

About three miles up the coast along the back lanes, via the village of Trefin, lies the narrow harbour inlet of Abercastle. Limited parking gives access to further rock ledges around the mouth of the harbour. The harbour has a narrow beachhead and a sand and shingle bottom but rougher ground can be located around and beyond the mouth. A couple of miles to the east-north-east are the twin beaches of Abermawr and Aberbach, with a small rocky bluff in between. Abermawr is the larger of the two and is reached by a short but fairly steep descent from the tiny roadside car park that leads onto its steep, north-west facing shingle bank. It is an impressive spot when a big onshore swell is running. The sea bed is mostly

Abercastle
*Abercastle's natural
harbour at high water*

Abermawr
*Abermawr has a
classic storm beach
which carries a good
surf in a NW wind*

Strumble Head
*Strumble Head's
clear waters are
well worth fishing in
settled conditions*

sand, with bouldery areas to either side. It has a bit of a mixed reputation, but with some water movement from a north-west breeze it has produced decent bass on occasion. Small flounders can be common, with pouting, whiting and dogfish all present, especially during the autumn and winter months.

Four miles to the north of Abermawr narrow lanes once again access the coast at Strumble Head, with its famous lighthouse. This area is hard-core rock country, with access for the fit and determined to rock platforms over very deep water indeed. The ground is typically rough and snaggy, with all that that implies for the angler seeking huss and conger. Lighter daytime fishing for wrasse and evening spinning for mackerel and pollack can both be worthwhile during the summer and early autumn, provided winds and swell are light and the weather is dry. It's a particularly impressive area when an autumn or winter storm is raging and the waves are breaking halfway up the cliffs!

Fishguard brings a complete change of scene, offering much more variety to the inexperienced and experienced angler alike. There are two long breakwaters that partly encircle the harbour where the ferry service over to Ireland is based. The longer western breakwater is open by arrangement only, access being limited to official angling clubs or during organised competition events. However, the shorter eastern one is freely accessible. Dealing with this venue first, there is a moderate depth of water off the end, but when choosing where to set up beware of the ropes from the numerous moorings and pot buoys in the vicinity. On a calm summer or autumn evening this is a great place to give a complete beginner a taste of fishing as the venue is often teeming with small pollack and wrasse close-in plus dogfish and a few flatfish further out. There are also whiting and pouting after dark, especially later in the year. The ground is rough close-in but clean sand is reached in no great distance.

The longer breakwater is an interesting venue. It is reinforced along the seaward side and around its end with huge rectangular concrete blocks. The deep, shady gaps in between these blocks are occupied by all sorts of small species including oddities like tadpole-fish. On the sheltered inside, a moderate cast finds deep water and mostly clean ground that can produce plenty of whiting at night in autumn and winter. Closer in it is very rough but that's where some big conger eels lurk. Summer sees pollack and mackerel take lures and float fished baits with dogfish, occasional huss, small whiting, pouting and flatfish also available.

Further marks are to be found in the area of Fishguard Old Town, where the old Harbour Quay offers relatively easy access to fairly clean ground. This mostly produces flounders, dogfish, pouting and whiting. Out along the coast path (accessed from the obvious bend and lay-by on the A487 just out of the town) is the Old Fort area where rock ledges offer lure and float fishing for mackerel, pollack and wrasse in season and dogfish, huss and other bottom feeders on larger baits cast out into the rough to mixed ground.

Eastwards to Dinas Head challenging rock country dominates. Just past Dinas Head is Cwm-yr-Eglwys, a small sandy cove flanked by rocks, with nearby parking. It's a beautiful spot which is, as a consequence, very popular – especially during the holiday season. Early mornings, late evenings and nights give the best chances. Fish off the beach or, in settled conditions, along the rocks to the west (left when facing the sea) where there are small platforms giving access to rough ground and deeper water. Dogfish and huss are frequent catches here, as are mackerel and pollack in the summer. Off the beach itself, flatfish, occasional bass, pouting, whiting and dogfish are the mainstays.

Newport Sands, just over two miles to the east, has a pleasant (and again popular) sandy beach with parking at the beachhead. The outfall of the estuary of the Nevern flows out across its western end. The beach faces north-west so a stiff breeze from that direction will bring on a decent surf, which will then make it worthwhile fishing for flounders and bass. Small-eyed rays are also possible, as are turbot – if the dogfish do not

Fishguard harbour
Fishguard harbour's two breakwaters seen from Goodwick. That on the right has unrestricted access but the left-hand one can only be accessed for official club events

Fishguard, Old Fort
On the eastern side of Fishguard, the Old Fort area offers rock fishing into fairly deep water

Cwm-yr-Eglwys
The small hamlet of Cwm-yr-Eglwys, starting point for exploring the area's many rock ledges

Newport beach – well worth fishing when it carries a bit of surf

find the necessary fish baits first! The estuary is fished for bass, flounders and mullet, all of which run up it on a flooding tide.

Beyond Newport, rock country again dominates, but there is one popular access point – Ceibwr Bay, near Moylegrove. Here, a narrow sandy cove is flanked to the east by towering cliffs, but to the west there are rock platforms and some deep gullies which are fishable provided conditions are not rough. Float fishing and spinning are the popular methods here – the targets being pollack, wrasse and mackerel. At night time, on the bottom in amongst the rough, huss, conger and the inevitable dogfish are also caught.

The final area in this section lies around Poppit Sands, along the south flank of the Teifi Estuary downstream from Cardigan. The river mouth is guarded by a beach and a shifting sand spit which gives both open beach and outer estuary fishing possibilities. Be careful if you venture out onto the sand spit and watch out that the incoming tide does not come round behind you. The outer beach produces similar species as Newport Sands – the estuary has bass, flounders and mullet. There is a sizeable channel in the estuary and fishing is best done either side of low water, when tidal currents are less strong. When the flow is at full bore it will tend to drape weed round your line and drag your rig into one of the many mooring ropes.

Ceibwr Bay – *near Moylgrove*

Poppit Sands – *where the Teifi flows into Cardigan Bay*

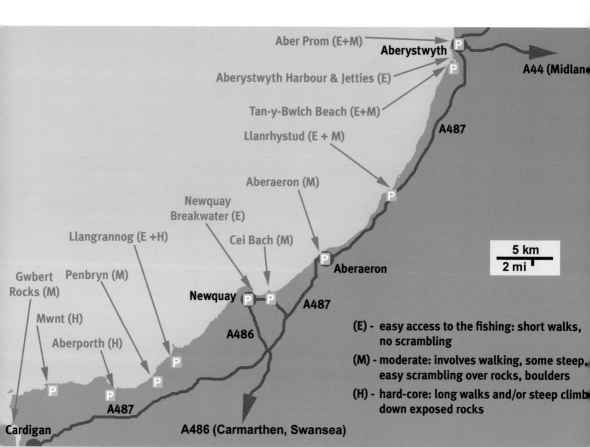

Aber Prom (E+M)

Aberystwyth

A44 (Midlan•

Aberystwyth Harbour & Jetties (E)

Tan-y-Bwlch Beach (E+M)

Llanrhystud (E + M)

A487

Aberaeron (M)

Newquay
Breakwater (E)

Cei Bach (M)

Aberaeron

Llangrannog (E +H)

Gwbert
Rocks (M)

Penbryn (M)

Newquay

A487

Mwnt (H)

A486

Aberporth (H)

A487

Cardigan

A486 (Carmarthen, Swansea)

5 km
2 mi

(E) - easy access to the fishing: short walks,
no scrambling

(M) - moderate: involves walking, some steep,
easy scrambling over rocks, boulders

(H) - hard-core: long walks and/or steep climb•
down exposed rocks

Cardigan to Aberystwyth
(the south-central section)

The southern part of this section is rock-bound but with several beautiful sandy beaches. Beyond Newquay, there is a change to mixed ground conditions with extensive bouldery beaches, sandy patches and, as Aberystwyth is approached, shallow rocky reefs. In addition there are breakwaters at Newquay, Aberaeron and Aberystwyth so there is something to suit most tastes and abilities.

There are access points to the north bank of the Teifi Estuary that offer similar fishing to the south bank mentioned previously. Continuing seawards, anglers who like a walk will find rock ledges below the Cliff Hotel at Gwbert, where the typical rough ground species can be targeted and bass, pollack and mackerel are caught on lures in season.

Mwnt
Late autumn sunset from a rock mark at Mwnt, near Cardigan

Mwnt is a narrow, sandy cove about three miles north-east of Cardigan. The beach is popular and there is a spacious car park. Anglers avoid the beach and head up over the hill north of the car park or eastwards along the coast path to fish rock platforms that are accessed by steep scrambling or in some cases climbing. These are strictly fair-weather marks for dry days with light winds and little or no swell. The marks to the east are particularly dangerous as they consist of rather smooth slabs dipping steeply straight down towards the sea. Following even the lightest rain, they become so slippery that

Mwnt to Aberporth
The Cardigan Bay coast from Mwnt (R) to Aberporth Head (L), with Cardigan Island in the background

Aberporth
The beach is small but there are worthwhile rock-ledges to the east to fish in settled conditions

movement across them becomes difficult and hazardous. The fishing is for all sorts of rough ground species close in, with longer casts finding sand and clean ground fish like whiting and dogfish. Mackerel and pollack are commonly taken on lures.

Further rock ledges are to be found east along the coastal footpath from Aberporth. These are popular as they are a noted spot for rays (mostly thornbacks) in the spring and autumn. Rough ground close-in gives way to clean sand at range – which is where the rays are located, along with dogfish, dabs and occasional plaice. Whiting are present in autumn and winter. Closer in, small rock dwelling species plus predators like huss and congers are on the list of possibilities, with mackerel and pollack to lures in the summer months.

North-eastwards from Aberporth's rocky coast a change is encountered with the first of a number of long, golden sandy beaches, commencing at Tresaith and running up to Penbryn, with parking and access at either of these points. In between, the beach is cliff-backed, with frequent caves present in the water-worn cliff bases. Bouldery patches are present in places. The rougher areas are preferred by bass fishermen who visit

in spring and autumn. During the day in summer the beach is crowded with sun worshippers, making fishing a night time or early morning occupation. Rays, flatfish and dogfish are all possibilities off the sand, with whiting in season. Weevers are also common here, so be sure to refer to the fish identification section of the book so that you can recognise one at a glance and avoid getting stung.

Continuing up the coast, a series of pleasant and popular sandy coves with rockier ground in between constitute the shore at Llangrannog. However, for the experienced and adventurous angler, the coastal path to the north-east leads towards Ynys Lochtyn, an elongated rocky island that can be accessed over low tide. Fishing here is a committing expedition possible only in settled conditions as it is necessary to go onto it at low water and come back off on the following low water some twelve hours later – hence the requirement to fully understand what the weather is going to do. The fishing is not dissimilar to that of the marks at previously-mentioned Mwnt

Penbryn Beach
Best fished at night
or outside the
holiday season

Llangrannog
*One of several sandy
coves at Llangrannog*

**North of
Llangrannog**
*The headland and
tidal island of Ynys
Lochtyn – a fair
weather expedition*

Newquay harbour
*The breakwater
is worth fishing
out of the holiday
season and at night.
Although it dries on
the inside, deeper
water is found along
its seaward flanks*

and Aberporth. The area has a huge spider crab population – at night, with a strong lamp, you can see them ambling around on the rock surfaces underwater. The last time I fished there I had a few mackerel at dusk but was utterly plagued with dogfish after dark, to the point that I gave up and dozed in my sleeping bag in a rocky niche high above the water until the morning low tide.

Newquay is a sizeable seaside resort and there are a number of fishing spots around the town's front (which faces north so offers a bit of shelter in south-westerly winds). The harbour breakwater is a relatively easy mark to approach and fish. It is a noted venue for dabs and whiting (plus, of course, dogfish) out over the sand, especially at night and during the autumnal months. Closer in amongst the rough there are all sorts of smaller species such as wrasse, blennies, small pollack and so on. Congers have also been taken in this rougher ground on occasion. Mackerel and garfish are targeted by float fishing during the summer months.

Just along the coast is Cei Bach (translates as Little Quay), which has a sweep of sand and, unseen beneath the waves, a reef producing a wide range of rock-loving species that good casters can reach at low tide. Mixed, boulder-strewn ground then becomes the norm all the way up past Aberaeron to

Cei Bach
The Ceredigion Sea-Anglers enjoying a March afternoon's fishing at Cei Bach beach, near Newquay

Llanrhystud and beyond. These two access points (and many in between, depending on fitness and enthusiasm), offer all the joys of mixed ground – with bass, huss and smooth hound possibilities in summer and codling in winter. They also offer all the challenges of such ground with frequent snags, abundant weed and terrain that is awkward underfoot due to the many boulders. Over the sandy patches, depending on the time of year, one can also expect bass, whiting, dabs, flounders, possible rays and dogfish. The short breakwater at Aberaeron offers little real advantage compared to the beach, but mackerel and garfish are targeted in its vicinity.

Northwards to Aberystwyth the often rocky coastline is backed by steep and crumbling cliffs with only the occasional access point, such as that adjacent to Morfa Bychan campsite. Mixed and shallow reef grounds dominate this section of the coast. Aberystwyth itself has a host of marks, some of which are very easy to reach and fish. From the sea front parking area south of the large harbour, there are four possibilities. From south to north, the first one is reached following a stiff walk along the wide shingle sweep of Tan-y-Bwlch Beach. At the southern end of the beach, low tide reveals a shallow, weed-strewn rocky reef, which, if you slip and slide to its edge, offers bass, wrasse and other species. The beach itself is more popular, feeling a lot safer underfoot! Its southern end offers mixed ground where conger and occasional huss are possible at night. Bass, mackerel, flounders, whiting, rays and dogfish are possible plus a good range of other species, along the whole beach.

The northern end of Tan-y-Bwlch beach is truncated by the Stone Jetty, a long stone and concrete breakwater, which is a popular and companionable mark, especially on a summer evening coinciding with high tide. On big tides its surrounding sea bed dries over low water for most of its length, so fishing is from mid-flood to mid-ebb. During this window of tidal opportunity, it is possible to fish on both sides, though if fishing on the north side into the busy harbour channel watch

Aberaeron
The easily-accessed South Beach at Aberaeron

Llanon
Shallow, stony ground continues north towards Llanon and Llanrhystud

Llanrhystud
Sandier conditions and easier access are to be found again at Llanrhystud

The Stone Jetty
Aberystwyth's Stone Jetty is a popular and sociable venue when the swell and winds are light

out for boats – they have the right of way here. Weed-covered boulders close in give way to sand and mud in the channel. Around the end of the breakwater and along the south side there are large, piled boulders for about forty yards and beyond that the ground is mostly clean, with localised rough patches. Out on the sand a range of species have been recorded over the years, of which dogfish, flounders, dabs, whiting and occasional gurnards are the most frequent. It can be rewarding to fish the bouldery area close-in with floats or by spinning for bass and, on summer early mornings and evenings, for mackerel, pollack and garfish. Bravely casting a large fish bait into the rough may tempt one of the large congers that lurk there. Smaller baits (typically ragworm) have produced an impressive range of species of which wrasse, blennies and sea scorpions are the most frequent. Just be mindful that it's a fair drop down to the sea and keep away altogether if there's a swell running – in such conditions huge waves will break right over the structure. If it's rough, fish the harbour instead.

The harbour has resident shoals of large mullet that can be seen cruising around when the water is clear. Flounders, small codling, bass, coalfish and eels have all been caught on legered baits – a popular spot is in front of the flats up to and over high tide. North of the harbour is the Wooden Jetty, smaller than its stone equivalent but with a not dissimilar range of species. Access is a short walk from the parking on the Prom, which also puts the town's beaches, and the shallow reefs between them, within reach. The beach fishing is similar to that on Tan-y-Bwlch Beach with some sizeable conger present close to the rockier areas and occasional good codling in winter. The beaches are of course thronged with holidaymakers during fine weather in the summer. The reefs are uncovered at low tide and are bisected by deep kelp-fringed gullies which offer short float fishing sessions for bass and wrasse from the slippery, weed-covered rock. Areas covered in barnacles offer the best footing.

Aberystwyth
Looking from Castle Point towards Constitution Hill, with the typical alternation of shallow rocky fingers and sandier bay

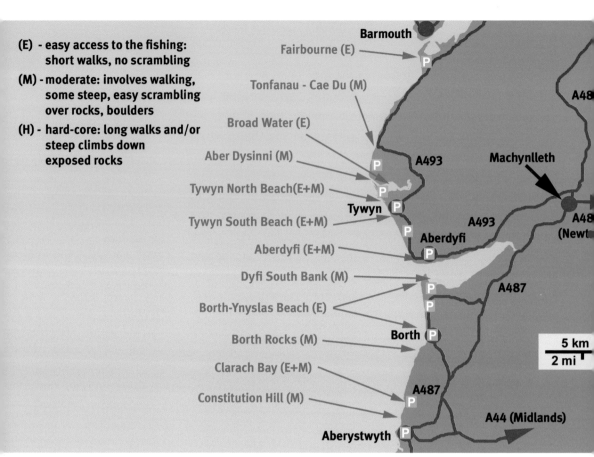

(E) - easy access to the fishing: short walks, no scrambling

(M) - moderate: involves walking, some steep, easy scrambling over rocks, boulders

(H) - hard-core: long walks and/or steep climbs down exposed rocks

Barmouth

Fairbourne (E)

Tonfanau - Cae Du (M)

Broad Water (E)

Aber Dysinni (M)

Tywyn North Beach (E+M)

Tywyn South Beach (E+M)

Aberdyfi (E+M)

Dyfi South Bank (M)

Borth-Ynyslas Beach (E)

Borth Rocks (M)

Clarach Bay (E+M)

Constitution Hill (M)

Aberystwyth

Tywyn

Aberdyfi

Borth

A493

A493

A487

A487

A48

A48 (Newt

Machynlleth

A44 (Midlands)

5 km
2 mi

Aberystwyth to Barmouth (the north-central section)

Most of this section of Cardigan Bay sees the change to very user-friendly territory as the shallow reefs north of Aberystwyth give way to long sandy beaches punctuated by occasional large estuaries and tracts of mixed ground and as a consequence it is much fished. Immediately north of Aberystwyth is Constitution Hill, with its cliff railway. Beneath 'Consti' (as locals refer to it), extensive gullied reefs stretch all the way to Clarach Bay, offering similar fishing to those along Aberystwyth Prom either side of low tide. Take care though not to get cut-off by the incoming tide! Clarach Bay has a cove of sand backed by shingle with a stream flowing into the sea. As you go further northwards shallow reef territory recommences interrupted by intermittent areas of mixed ground (such as Sarn Cynfelyn's boulder bank), right up to Borth. Immediately south of Borth the rocks are popular in summer with people trying to catch prawns in the rock pools. In places these reefs offer access at low tide to clean ground at range, but the most popular fishing is for bass, either by float fishing or spinning – with mackerel and garfish in season too. Legering fish baits at night can produce small congers but swarms of dogfish are often also in attendance.

Borth Beach consists of several miles of clean sand, with areas of peat studded with tree trunks – the so-called 'Submerged Forest'. This feature, best seen after winter storms scour away a lot of sand, is up to 6,500 years old and marks a time when sea levels were lower and the waterline some distance away to the west. The beach carries a good surf and is very popular with water sports enthusiasts and holidaymakers alike. Fish in spring, autumn or winter, at night or first thing in the morning in the summer – it's a pleasant spot capable of producing bass, rays (mostly small-eyed), dabs, flounders and turbot. Mackerel sometimes work the beach during summer and autumn evenings. Dogfish can be abundant at night during spring and autumn.

Sarn Cynfelyn
The unusual boulder ridge of Sarn Cynfelyn, between Aberystwyth and Borth,
viewed from the Coastal Path. The shore hereabouts is mixed ground with large sandy patches between the more bouldery areas

Ynyslas Dunes mark the top end of the beach, where it meets the expansive Dyfi Estuary. From the parking on the flat sands, estuary fishing is possible on the second half of the ebb down to low water and back up the first half of the flood. Big spring tides cover the parking area at high water. Where you fish depends on how far you want to walk. Fishing is primarily for bass and flounders, with evenings, nights or early morning preferred – the jet skiers are tucked-up in bed then! Muddy creeks such as the outfall of the Leri often reveal shoals of good-sized mullet too. These marks are safe so long as one stays on terra firma, avoiding the shifting sandbanks that appear at low water, which are, in patches, very soft underfoot.

Aberdyfi, on the Dyfi estuary's northern side, is a very popular spot in summer with a great deal of boating activity. However, at quieter times of year or early in the morning and late in the evening, it offers access to the main channel of the estuary after a short trudge across the sand from the waterfront parking. The channel offers spinning for bass and garfish around low water, with conventional bait fishing either side of low water on any tide and in pretty much any weather. On the full force of the tide at mid-flood, the current can bring with it floating weed, fouling lines and making fishing unpleasant.

During smaller neap tides, though, the spot can fish well over high water, especially later in the year when bass, flounders, dabs, whiting, dogfish and even codling are possible. Lesser weevers are common over these sandy grounds, especially those around the town's wooden jetty, which can be extremely busy with families hand-lining in among its timber supports for crabs. Sand smelts and sandeels are also caught here by anglers seeking fresh bait by jigging light lures. Just be sure to check out the fish identification section of this book so that if you catch a weever you know what you are dealing with.

North of the mouth of the Dyfi, another long sandy beach begins, with the fishing (and water sports scene) very similar to that at Borth. This area is accessed from Aberdyfi, Tywyn

The Dyfi Estuary
A wide expanse of clean sand interspersed with stony, weedy patches

Tywyn
*The ideal time to fish
Tywyn's main beach
– after sundown*

and a car park/footpath in between the two, although except at Tywyn, a good walk is required. Off the Prom at Tywyn the beach takes on a steeper angle, with large bouldery reefs at and below the low tide mark, plus some modern artificial ones, constructed in recent years to protect the town from storm-damage. It is a good night time venue for whiting and occasional codling in autumn and winter, with dogfish also in abundance at times. Pouting, rockling, flounders, dabs and turbot are also regular catches as are bass and small-eyed rays, with black bream possible in late summer. There is a particularly strong south to north flow here on the early flood which can make life trying if there is much weed in the water, but these problems tend to ease off higher in the tide, unless conditions are really bad.

The beach continues in a similar fashion all the way up to the stony mouth of Afon Dysynni, the latter being a popular spot for fly and lure anglers who carefully wade out on fine evenings after the bass. The river mouth is accessible most of the time by parking and walking seawards under the railway bridge, except for the time around high water on the bigger tides. On such tides, bass (and sometimes garfish) can run upriver beyond the bridge. Mullet are common and are often fished for in the tidal lagoon of Broadwater, which is situated a short distance upstream from the bridge.

North of the Dysynni is the start of a lengthy tract of mixed ground, consisting of acres of tackle-grabbing, weedy boulders, with occasional sandy patches. This extends up past the popular campsite of Cae-Du to Llwyngwril and beyond to the southern end of Fairbourne Beach. Access points at Tonfanau, Cae-Du and Llwyngwril make it possible, with a certain amount of walking, to locate fishable spots over low water. Bass, huss and dogfish are the mainstays, but there are other possibilities – the Welsh record monkfish was taken at Llwyngwril some years ago and codling ought to be present in winter. The mixed ground gives way to sand again at Friog, where Fairbourne Beach begins, with a return to the type of fishing found at Borth and between Aberdyfi and Tywyn. The Mawddach estuary's south bank (opposite Barmouth), fishes similarly to the Dyfi Estuary at Ynyslas.

North of Tywyn
The sweep of storm beach north of Tywyn

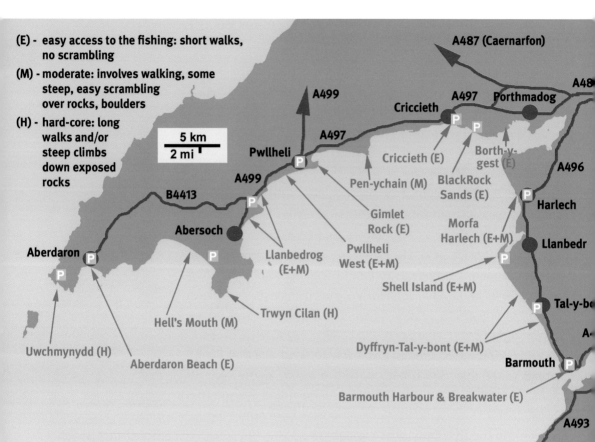

(E) - easy access to the fishing: short walks, no scrambling

(M) - moderate: involves walking, some steep, easy scrambling over rocks, boulders

(H) - hard-core: long walks and/or steep climbs down exposed rocks

5 km
2 mi

A487 (Caernarfon)

A48

A499

A497 Porthmadog

Criccieth

A497

Pwllheli

Criccieth (E)

Borth-y-gest (E)

A496

A499

Pen-ychain (M)   BlackRock Sands (E)

B4413

Harlech

Gimlet Rock (E)

Morfa Harlech (E+M)

Abersoch

Pwllheli West (E+M)

Llanbedrog (E+M)

Aberdaron

Shell Island (E+M)

Llanbedr

Trwyn Cilan (H)

Tal-y-bo

Hell's Mouth (M)

A

Uwchmynydd (H)

Dyffryn-Tal-y-bont (E+M)

Aberdaron Beach (E)

Barmouth

Barmouth Harbour & Breakwater (E)

A493

Barmouth to Bardsey Sound (the north-west section)

User-friendly fishing continues right up this coast to the crook of Cardigan Bay at Porthmadog and beyond to Criccieth. Access points are busy areas and the angler prepared to walk a bit will find quieter sections away from the crowds. From Pwllheli westwards the fishing gets progressively more challenging with alternating rocky headlands and storm beaches until the hard-core rock fishing area of Bardsey Sound, to the south-west of Aberdaron, is reached.

Barmouth is a popular and busy coastal resort with a harbour area in an enclave on the north side of the Mawddach estuary – to the east is the railway bridge over the estuary and seaward, to the west, a short breakwater. The breakwater and

bridge both offer access to the deeper main channel – check locally to make sure of the current access situation with the bridge. Another important point if you fish the bridge, is to consider how you might get a large bass up from the surface of the water to your stance many feet above! The breakwater is a simple three hundred yard trek from the large car park on the Prom although there are venues within the harbour itself if a shorter walk is preferred. The fishing is similar in all areas – the main channel is rough in places, but spinning off the end of the breakwater above the snags can be successful when the bass and garfish are feeding. Apart from bass and garfish, the venues offer similar species to the Dyfi Estuary – flounders, occasional plaice and mullet, with dabs, whiting and dogfish in autumn and winter. Weevers can be abundant, so be careful.

North of the harbour area, there's a long tract of sandy, shingle-backed beach having access points at spots like Llanaber, Dyffryn and Tal-y-bont, with miles of shallow surf to explore in between. Fish nights or early mornings in the height

Barmouth
Barmouth harbour and the Cambrian Coast railway bridge from the breakwater – a popular venue especially in the summer

of the holiday season to avoid the crowds. Bass, flounders, rays and turbot from the middle of spring onwards are joined by dabs and whiting in the autumn and winter with (as usual) frequent dogfish, of course!

A break in the sands occurs at Shell Island or Mochras, where a broad point of mixed ground pushes out into the bay. The south-western side of the point sees the clean sand beach that stretches away southwards making a transition to mixed, bouldery ground. The sands are thronged with holidaymakers at peak season, meaning fishing is only worthwhile at night or early in the morning, but the bouldery ground is quieter and, despite its forbidding appearance, can nevertheless fish well over localised sandy patches, located via a recce at low water. Bass, dogfish and huss plus flatfish and rays over sandier areas and mullet in the river mouth form the mainstays, with late season whiting at night and mackerel and garfish in the summer months when the weather is settled.

North of the Artro Estuary sandy conditions are resumed just beyond the stony but easily accessed shore at Llandanwg. The sandy sweep runs all the way up past Harlech to the southern side of the estuary of Afon Glaslyn, opposite Porthmadog. Access to the water's edge involves a short walk from the beach car park at Harlech, but from here up to the estuary it is a trudge of over two miles each way, so it should be fairly quiet up there! The fishing is similar to that found between Barmouth and Shell Island.

The beautiful Glaslyn estuary has easier access from Borth-y-gest, due south of Porthmadog, where the Glaslyn is joined by Afon Dwyryd in a maze of winding channels and sand bars. Bass, flounders and mullet (plus weevers) are the main species here, targeted from a number of points along the coast path. Dogfish and whiting will invade the main channels on night tides later in the year.

One of the busiest beaches in Wales (because cars are allowed onto it by day) commences beyond the estuary mouth. This is the famous Black Rock Sands, the Black Rock being the

Shell Island
The point at Mochras (Shell Island), where sand meets boulders

North of Mochras
From the point at Mochras to Llandanwg, it's rough and stony but there are sandy patches to be found at low tide

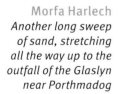

Morfa Harlech
Another long sweep of sand, stretching all the way up to the outfall of the Glaslyn near Porthmadog

Borth-y-gest
*The Glaslyn Estuary
at Borth-y-gest*

prominent outcrop at the western end. Impossible to fish when crowded, it is nevertheless worth a go at the estuary mouth around low tide, early in the morning or late in the evening, when other beach goers have departed.

Criccieth is the next ready access point and here the ground starts to change to a more mixed type, the fishing also changing accordingly – with wrasse, pollack (mostly small) and occasional huss over the rougher areas accompanying bass, dogfish and dabs over the sandy areas. Just east of the ancient ruined castle is a short stone jetty which can be fished when conditions are settled – with clean ground straight off the end for the flatfish and rough ground towards the castle. On the western side of the castle headland a short tract of clean ground quickly gives way to mixed territory again, with a similar range of fish.

Beyond Criccieth similar but less accessible ground continues on westwards beyond the mouth of Afon Dwyfor and the angler who enjoys a good walk will find plenty of spots to explore. The coast juts out at Pen-ychain and is accessible along public paths through/past the Butlin's holiday camp, forming a handy mark for anglers staying there. This low, rocky point gives access to slightly deeper water – as well as bass, flatfish and dogfish (sometimes in vast numbers), a variety of other species have been recorded here, among them huss to a good size and black bream.

Bream feature right along the next section of coast, from Abererch through Pwllheli to Llanbedrog. The most accessible points are at Pwllheli – from east to west these are the Marina

Black Rock Sands
The view westwards at low tide beyond the Black Rock to Criccieth and the castle

Channel, Gimlet Rock, the Prom and the Golf Course – all of which can give fishing with just a short walk. Black bream show at all of these marks, with some decent specimens having been recorded amongst the more general run of smaller fish. Some good bream have been taken from the busy channel leading from the Marina which, owing to boat traffic, is a dusk and dawn venue. Bass, flounders and mullet can also be expected here. Gimlet Rock is the prominent rock outcrop at the east end of the main beach. It and the beach to its west give access to slightly deeper water and mainly clean ground with patches of rough and dense beds of eelgrass. It is good for variety at times except after rough weather when

Pwllheli

A deserted Pwllheli Beach from Gimlet Rock, late on a winter afternoon

Carreg-y-Defaid

This is one of several rocky points along the coastline between Criccieth and Llanbedrog, giving access to only slightly deeper water in this shallow part of Cardigan Bay

Abersoch
The beach is shallow and tends to be busy. Early mornings and late evenings along the Warren beach to the east, which runs up to the quarried headland that separates it from Llanbedrog, are better

rafts of floating eelgrass can drape lines like so much laundry. As well as bream, bass, dogfish, dabs and whiting it can produce thornback and spotted rays, especially at night in the spring, plus huss, occasional tope, gurnards and oddities like dragonets and red mullet. Mackerel and garfish are common in the summer when the weather is settled.

Similar conditions are to be found along to the Prom and the Golf Course – the main difference being that the water becomes shallower the further west one goes. Bream, bass and dogfish are caught all along this stretch and beyond towards Llanbedrog, where stingrays have been recorded in early summer. Beyond the next steep headland is the Warren Beach, a clean stretch of sand heading westwards towards Abersoch. Backed by caravan-sites, it is very busy in the holiday season which means, for the sake of sanity, fishing at night, very early in the morning or outside of the holiday season. The beach has pretty much the whole range of Welsh flatfish, with bass, dogfish and whiting in the autumn.

Abersoch itself has one of the busiest boating scenes anywhere in Wales. Consequently anglers thereabouts tend to escape to the relative peace of the hard-core rock marks and storm beaches further west again. The first such rock mark is

Trwyn Cilan, a large headland three miles south-south-west of Abersoch, with a strenuous approach demanding skill in handling steep rock and heights and no place to be in rough sea conditions or in the wet. In settled weather there are ledges from which pollack and mackerel are taken on lures whilst baits find good huss, conger, big ballan wrasse and other species.

Hell's Mouth
*West of Abersoch,
and seen here in
unusually quiet mood*

Beyond Trwyn Cilan is Hell's Mouth, a long gently curved sweep of storm beach which is reached via the village of Llanengan and a sign-posted lane to parking some five minutes' walk from the sea. When it's a bit rough elsewhere it's really rough here (hence the name), but in a good steady surf it can fish well for bass and flatfish. Rock country then intervenes once more, with headlands such as Trwyn Talfarach (near Rhiw) and Trwyn y Penrhyn to the west, again requiring walking and scrambling with steep sections in places. Preliminary reconnaissance is again advised in order to find the best spots to be fished safely when settled weather conditions permit. Parking is offered at some of the farms and it shortens the walk – best to ask locally when you are there to ascertain the current situation. In between the headlands are rocky coves with short stretches of boulders and sand, such as Porth Ysgo, which are home

Penarfynydd
Beyond Hell's Mouth it's mostly rock country, including the steep headland of Penarfynydd, near Rhiw

Porth Ysgo
The sand bottomed cove of Porth Ysgo, with the old manganese mine remains on the cliff top

Aberdaron
*The sandy sweep of
Aberdaron Beach
– the last beach on
the Cardigan Bay
Coast. Like the first,
Whitesands Bay, it's
very busy by day*

to bass and a variety of mixed ground species depending on
how close to rougher areas you cast. Beyond this section, the
next and last sweep of sand on the Cardigan Bay Coast is
reached at Aberdaron, which is similar (but a bit gentler) in
nature to Hell's Mouth. With a popular pub fronting the beach
and local boat launching facilities, it is understandably busy by
day. When there's some surf running, fish it during evenings,
nights and early mornings, especially in autumn and winter,
when the bass and flatties will move in to feed. On a sunny
summer afternoon, the best bet is to grab a pint and laze away
an hour enjoying the scenery.

Winding lanes beyond Aberdaron lead to Uwchmynydd
and the steep, craggy coastline that faces Bardsey Sound
– a serious bit of water through which the tides surge in
spectacular fashion at five knots or more on springs. Marks
along this last bit of the Cardigan Bay Coast all require a good
walk and access is in some cases very strenuous – to the
extent that one spot is affectionately known to its devotees as
'Cardiac Hill'. Some marks require a steady head for heights,
good route finding and in places climbing (rather than just
scrambling) ability. These are strictly fair weather venues only
– no rain, no strong winds and little swell. When conditions

are good, they provide fit and experienced anglers with good lure fishing for pollack, mackerel and coalfish where headlands jut out to create tide-rips. In between the headlands there are deep inlets with rough craggy seabeds where bait-fishing for huss, conger, large wrasse and lots of smaller species is possible, especially over smaller neap tides when the current is not so strong. Finishing as it started, on a rocky note, this concludes our itinerary around Cardigan Bay.

Bardsey Sound
Rock-bound all the way with demanding approaches to many marks, but in settled weather the fishing can be rewarding

The Fish Species
of the Cardigan Bay coast

This chapter does not cover every single species of fish that inhabits the Cardigan Bay shoreline. Some are too small to catch on rod and line, while at the other end of the spectrum there is the giant, plankton-eating filter-feeder, the basking shark, occasionally sighted from the shore. In between these extremes are the many species of fish that I and other local anglers have caught over the past decades, some on a regular basis and others occasional or one-off catches.

The chapter is in two parts. Firstly, I take a look at the key families of fish and their members in detail, explaining how and when to target them. Secondly, for identification purposes, I have taken or in a few cases obtained images of a wider range of species, complete with essential, at-a-glance information. Many of the images were taken during my 2008 quest to catch 30 species from the Welsh shore in a year, followed up in 2009 by a more ambitious target of 40, a challenge which was successfully achieved in the middle of December of that year.

Species hunting has become a popular branch of sea angling that brings a lot of new thinking and refinements in tactics to one's water-craft. It can also become a burning obsession, as evidenced by the fact that in December 2009, having been pinned down for weeks by relentless autumn gales, I visited three venues over two days just to get a five-bearded rockling! The first session on December 10th at Aberystwyth was wrecked by a big swell threatening to break over the Stone Jetty and the second, at Tywyn that evening, by dense floating weed. Time was running out, but on the evening of the 11th, sea conditions had improved markedly and I returned to the Stone Jetty, landing seven species in a couple of hours including two five-bearded rocklings. Species number 40 was in the bag:

Opposite:
The author
John Mason with a fine bass

never has a five-bearded rockling been greeted with so much enthusiasm, before or since.

The second part also gives current Welsh shore-caught records for each species in case you catch a potential record-breaker and additionally it notes minimum sizes in order to avoid taking undersized specimens. The Welsh Federation of Sea Anglers (WFSA) is the body that maintains the record list and deals with new record claims via its website at www. wfsa.org.uk. With respect to retaining fish, in some cases the minimum size is a matter of law whilst in others the WFSA has issued guidelines that all anglers are advised to follow: in such cases the minimum sizes are annotated (WFSA).

BASS

When I began sea angling in the very early 1980s, it seemed to be generally accepted (and often printed) wisdom that bass were unlikely, with a few noted exceptions, to be encountered north of a line from Anglesey to Humberside. Today, the picture is very different – just as one example among many, they have been regularly caught in recent years by anglers undertaking the time-honoured activity of spinning for sea-trout on Orkney. Likewise, they are no longer regarded as limited in their occurrence to the warmer months and in mild winters I have caught bass in the dark depths of January. However, despite the lengthening season and expanding northward range of the species, the best catches around Cardigan Bay still occur primarily from April to November.

Bass are unmistakable – bright silver in colour (larger older specimens have black backs), with an upright spiny dorsal fin that you will get spiked by if careless. The gill covers each carry a very sharp bony plate too, as many have found out the hard way! Small bass, up to a couple of pounds or so, go around in shoals, and that's why you may hear the term 'school bass' or 'schoolies'. Bigger bass tend to be loners and there is some evidence that they are rather territorial in nature. Slow growing fish, they take four years to reach the Welsh legal minimum keeping size of 14.7 inches (37.5cm). At this size, they may not have yet bred and I would therefore suggest adopting the WFSA suggested minimum of 17.7 inches (45cm). Let them have one go first! A double-figure bass can be over 20 years old, will invariably be a female and should be regarded as prime spawning stock. Although some anglers keep larger bass for eating, I have found examples from 3 to 6lb to be the best eaters. I put the rarer big specimens back.

Let's look at standard bait fishing first. Tackle-wise, leger rigs are ideal. Medium gauge hooks are required at sizes from 1/0 up to 6/0 depending on the type and size of the bait. Fine wire hooks should be avoided as they can spring open when a big bass takes savagely and 25lb hook-lengths are as strong as you need to go: in clear, daylight conditions many anglers fish much lighter. Generally, baits should be fished on the bottom, which is where the foraging bass will be looking for food. However, being active predators, they will snap at things in mid water too, which is why lures, which we will come to shortly, are so effective. In May 2011, I had a six-pounder take a washed-out crab bait in mid water on the retrieve. I must have reeled it virtually past the nose of the fish as the water was quite cloudy. But it's the only one I have caught like that in 30 years of catching them, so I guess it was a bit unusual.

A more frequent take will be a 'slack-liner' – if you've not been concentrating and then turn to your rod to see the line hanging limply from its tip, grab it and reel in like mad. The fish has taken the bait, hooked itself and has run towards you, towing the sinker behind it. If you're lucky, it may still be on! I have had bass hit like this a hundred yards out and have only caught up with them twenty yards from the water's edge.

Gradually rising sea temperatures and longer daylight lead to increasingly more bass making their way into our inshore waters in March. The trickle becomes a flood between April and mid-May, depending on the weather conditions. The reason for that is simple: the first big 'crab peel' of the year, triggered itself, among other things, by rising temperatures. This process creates a lot of scent in the water and as crabs can only mate when the female has peeled and has a completely soft body, hormones are released too. As a consequence, the bass know when the peel has started and they invade crab-rich areas such as reefs, mixed ground beaches and estuaries to feast on the moulted individuals. At this time of year, they are so preoccupied with munching crabs that other baits will rarely score.

By summertime, an abundance of alternative food sources will be available inshore such as prawns, sandeels, whitebait and, for the bigger fish, mackerel. In early Autumn whiting and pouting can be added to the menu. Thus, at these times, fish baits like sandeels, mackerel fillets, whole pouting and squid are effective. Along the shallow reefs, summertime float fishing in the gullies with prawns is a traditional and often deadly method. In autumn, storms wash out worms and shellfish from sandbanks and baits such as lugworm and razor come into their own along the surf-beaches and in nearby estuaries. The art of bass fishing with bait is to anticipate what food items the fish will be expecting to find as they hunt and provide them with an appropriate portion.

This anticipation of fish-behaviour works on another level, too: the fact that bass respond well to lures allows the angler to completely dispense with bait and the hassle and expense of obtaining it. Bass are caught on lures pretty much all year round, though catches are most consistent during the summer and autumn months when the fish are preoccupied with feeding on fry, as opposed to their annual springtime obsession with seeking out soft crabs. Lure fishing is something of a liberation. It allows one to dispense with the heavy seat-box full of rigs and sinkers. Wandering freely with a light rod and reel, a small pocket-sized box of lures and another containing spare swivels, line and a few light weights, the lure angler can explore long sections of the coastline unburdened. Indeed, an important attribute of the successful lure angler is to be prepared to move around, working as much of the water as possible in order to find the fish. Sometimes, this task is made easier when the bass are feeding close to the surface, causing swirls and splashes. At other times they are deeper: in such circumstances, many lure anglers wear polaroid sunglasses to improve the odds of spotting the fish. Watch out for diving terns and other seabirds as these will be feeding where the baitfish are congregated, as will any bass that are in the area.

Terns diving
If you want to know where the baitfish are, follow the seabirds

Lures come in many shapes and sizes, which can be a bit confusing for the beginner. However, the important point to remember is that so long as they resemble the fish that the bass are preoccupied with, they should produce the goods. Sandeels are a major food item, occurring in abundance in almost every inshore environment, and it is no coincidence that soft lures that resemble them can be deadly for bass. Of the myriad soft lures on the market, a personal favourite is the 'Slug-go', because when rigged with a special 'Texposer' hook, which sits with the hook-point flush against the upper body of the lure, it very rarely picks up any floating weed. In estuaries and over mixed ground, where the water is rarely weed-free, that can make the difference between being able to fish or not. It also produces savage takes.

Other soft sandeel impersonations worth trying include the original Eddystone Eels and Red Gills, proven fish-catchers of many years' pedigree, through to the more recent models like Sidewinders and Berkley Gulp lures. Size and colour are important considerations. Ideally, your lure will be a similar size to the sandeels that the fish are feeding on. If, for example, you notice shoals of four- to six-inch sandeels in the water, choose a lure in that size range. Experienced lure anglers with detailed knowledge of their favourite marks will have developed this knowledge through time. Colour determines the visibility of the lure to the fish, something that also varies depending on water clarity. In very clear water, I prefer to use a lure in 'natural' colours: the fish can see it clearly and the more it looks and behaves like a real prey item, the better. Pale colours are also good in such circumstances. When the water is a bit coloured, black lures score well as they create a strong silhouette against the sky, giving the fish the best chance of actually seeing the lure.

Soft lures can be used close-in unweighted and some actually come with built-in weight for added casting distance. Others need to be rigged with a sinker for fishing at range. I rig them leger-style, with a drilled bullet threaded onto the main line, followed by a knot-cushioning bead before the swivel and three-foot hook-length. The amount of weight depends on how far you want to cast, but a one-ounce bullet gives a decent range when using light spinning tackle. Another way of weighting a soft lure during the cast is to use a bubble float filled with water or a rubber 'bouncyball' with a hole drilled through the middle. The big advantage here is that due to the buoyancy of the 'weight', the lure stays up in the water during the retrieve, something that may be vital to success when spinning shallow water over a snaggy, tackle-grabbing seabed.

Once the lure has been cast out, retrieve it in the general direction of the tidal flow, slowly and steadily. This will optimise the chances of a bass spotting the lure and following it, perhaps to mount its attack. There are few angling experiences more heart-stopping than retrieving a lure and seeing a bass looming up, sometimes taking at the last minute or sometimes veering away, realising that it has been deceived.

An equally diverse range of hard lures is available on the market, but of all these, my favourite is the 'Dexter Wedge' family. There are several reasons for this preference. Firstly, in weights up to a couple of ounces it can be cast a long way, a useful property at many venues. Secondly, its action is excellent: it flutters and wobbles its way through the water, giving off vibrations that the bass will sense and home in on as they would with a wounded baitfish. Thirdly, the bright metallic colour gives off flashes of colour that the fish will detect from some distance in clear conditions. For shorter ranges, lighter spoons like the Toby are also excellent in terms of action and visibility. As a general consideration, the more slimline versions of these lures will cast better if you have a headwind to deal with. In all cases, a slow, steady retrieve as described for soft lures is the most effective way of provoking a take.

Plug fishing for bass has developed something of a cult status over recent years. These relatively expensive but deadly lures come in a variety of designs that affect their behaviour. Some have a single body, others a jointed body that increases movement and vibration. Some contain beads that give off a rattle as they are worked through the water. The concave-faced surface poppers are perfect for fishing over snag-ridden ground where the bass use rocks and weed to wait in ambush. Where conditions are less snaggy, shallow to deep-diving plugs may be used: the depth at which these fish is determined by the shape of the front of the head or by the angle at which the diving-vane is set – the closer to vertical it is the shallower it will fish. However, plugging with a surface popper, such as the 'Storm Chug-bug', is one of the most exciting ways to fish for bass, the lure skipping and splashing its way across the surface just like a baitfish frantically trying to get to safety as the bass looms up behind it, creating a bow wave as it moves in to attack. It is important to realise that each plug will have its own individual action that the angler has to bring out by the way in which the lure is retrieved: for example, a popper is made to create small splashes by flicking the rod tip to speed it up and slow it down as the line is wound in. This is very definitely a case of 'practice makes perfect'.

When very small fry are on the menu for the bass, which is often the case in estuaries or around reefs, they can go into such a feeding-frenzy that they can be caught on feathers, like mackerel. On occasion I've been briefly mislead into thinking the mackerel have arrived in this way, with the sea boiling and small whitebait frantically leaping clear. These tend to be smaller school bass: the bigger ones, with years of experience behind them, are more wily. However, well-designed flies will still fool these fish, as Paul's section on saltwater flyfishing has explained.

One mark I fish on occasion is a bridge over a small tidal river. The bass run upstream on the flood and come back down on the ebb, when standing by the upstream parapet of the bridge, dropping a lure in, paying out a little line and letting it flutter slowly downstream in the current can sometimes produce. Once, I hooked a four-pounder on a silver Toby lure – the fish took off and went straight around behind the downstream bridge parapet, where it moved back and forth, the line taut and audibly rubbing on the stonework. It was almost as if it had figured it could wear the line through with this applied abrasion. Realising I was fast running out of options, I applied maximum pressure – it was a 'bass or bust' situation. I was lucky – the fish shot back upstream and was out in front of me in deeper water, where it was landed quickly.

Over the years I've caught bass on pretty much every bait imaginable, on many types of lure, by leger or by float. All in all, the fact that they are at home in such a variety of Cardigan Bay's marine ecosystems and can be caught by such a range of tactics and baits, makes them a very worthwhile target for beginner and experienced angler alike.

BREAMS

The sea breams are an extensive family of fish that are widely distributed around the warmer seas of the world. In Cardigan Bay, three species are known, of which just one, the black bream, is relatively common. The other two, the gilthead and the red bream, are very infrequent captures, although there is anecdotal evidence that giltheads are slowly increasing in numbers. This would be a welcome trend if we end up with the good numbers of giltheads that visit the Cornish tidal creeks every summer, where knowledgeable locals catch them on worm and crab baits.

The black bream is easy to identify – it is a deep-bodied fish, silvery with a purplish tint and sometimes with vertical darker bars along its flanks. They grow to around 5lbs in size but a shore caught fish of 2lb would be regarded as a good specimen by most. It is also easy to tell the difference between a gilthead and a black bream as although they are similar in colour, the gilthead has a band of gold across the 'forehead', above the eyes.

Bream inhabit rocky and weedy areas – boulder reefs and eelgrass beds are favourite breeding and feeding habitats. Boat anglers enjoy good fishing over the Sarnau – the extensive bouldery reefs in central Cardigan Bay. For the shore angler, it is a matter of locating favourable areas and putting in the time. Some of the most reliable bream fishing is at marks in the Pwllheli area, where the eelgrass meadows flourish just off the beach. Even these marks seem to blow hot and cold, fishing well one day and quiet the next. One trick that can improve the odds in your favour when fishing amongst this bootlace-like weed is to incorporate floating beads into your hook-length. You can either buy these or fashion your own from polystyrene 'worms' used in parcel-packaging. Floating beads will lift the baited hooks up in the water, so that they bob about above the eelgrass, making them easier for the fish to spot. If using high visibility baits like small strips cut from the belly of a mackerel, this method will also catch bonus sight-feeding predators like mackerel or garfish.

Bream have small mouths so baits and hooks need to be small. Size 2 to 4 hooks, baited with worms, strips of squid, peeler crab, small mackerel strips or shellfish and fished on 2 or 3-hook paternoster rigs do the trick – 25lb hook-lengths, 6 to12 inches long, are ideal. Bream seem to be quite faddy when it comes to feeding and during boat fishing sessions, when several anglers are using a variety of baits, I have noted that they can show distinct preferences on different days – one day it might be squid, on another bits of ragworm and on another cockles, of all things. On the right bait you get take after take as soon as the rig hits the bottom, whilst on other baits catches are much reduced. Why? I don't know, but what I do know is that carrying some of each of these baits maximises your chances of catching on any given day.

COD FAMILY – overview

In UK waters, members of the cod family make up many of the catches of shore and boat anglers alike. Eleven species are deliberately targeted or accidentally caught by the Cardigan Bay shore angler. These comprise the cod itself, whiting, pouting, poor cod, tadpole-fish, pollack, coalfish, the three rocklings and ling. A twelfth, the haddock, is a very remote possibility from the deepest marks in the far NW and SW.

Cod

The Welsh stronghold of the cod is without doubt the Bristol Channel, with Cardigan Bay widely regarded as a poor second cousin in that respect. However, some are caught in the late autumn and winter months from the deeper marks – from rocky ground, steep shingle beaches and estuary channels. In summer, boat anglers take a few from the inshore reefs most years and the shore catches may well represent these localised reef populations moving closer in to feed. Anything over 5lb is generally regarded as a very good Cardigan Bay specimen from the shore. Although the legal minimum size for cod is 13.7 inches (35cm), they have such large heads that such a fish would have little to eat on it. Like many legal minimum sizes, this figure should be regarded as a bare minimum.

The best tactics in Cardigan Bay for cod involve a similar approach to that taken for autumn bass – big baits consisting of what is appropriate at the time. If it has been stormy, razor and lugworm baits do well. In more settled conditions, squid works and I have had them on mackerel baits intended for whiting, too. Crab baits can produce them in rocky and weedy areas and they also feed heavily on the smaller species of their own family (like whiting and rockling), that move in close to shore on night-tides. My personal best from the Bay was caught at Tywyn, just before Christmas in 2003 – it took a whole five-bearded rockling and weighed 6.5 lbs. Big baits require big hooks, and a sharp, strong 6/0 is ideal. Take a second rod along and fish for other species like whiting, as cod catches are not guaranteed.

Whiting

As autumn arrives, whiting invade Cardigan Bay's inshore waters in large numbers, congregating and feeding primarily over sandy ground. The legal minimum size is just 10.6 inches (27 cm) and hereabouts a fish of over a pound can be regarded as a good one. Despite being small fish, what they lack in size they make up for in numbers. On a calm frosty night over high tide they keep the angler busy (and thereby warm) with their frequent knocking bites. Rough weather tends to see the whiting move out a little, out of harm's way, but they will swiftly return once the sea fines down following a blow. They are tasty when eaten fresh provided you gut them quickly after death. While whiting will eat just about anything, fish baits like strips of mackerel and herring seem to sort out the better ones, as do sections of sandeel. Two or three-hook paternoster rigs, fitted with 25lb hook-lengths and armed with size 2 up to 1/0 long-shanked fine wire hooks will allow you to bag up if they are there in good numbers.

Whiting have sharp little teeth and will often rip apart large baits intended for bigger fish. I was once treated to a fascinating example of the gluttony that this fish is sometimes inclined towards. There had been a big late winter storm with winds of Violent Storm Force 11 coinciding with a spring tide and once it had blown over I headed to Borth beach at low water to see if anything of interest had been washed up. Weed, clams, driftwood and other debris littered the sands, and walking along filling my bait bucket with clams I was amazed to come across several dead foot-long whiting, each with a corkwing wrasse tail protruding from its mouth. The huge storm waves that had battered the reef south of Borth must have killed a few of the resident wrasse, their bodies floating around until the whiting had found them and attempted to swallow them whole, head first. This being a rather over-ambitious prospect, the wrasse had become firmly jammed in the whiting's gullets, leading to their demise. It was one of those occasions where I wished I had taken a camera along!

Pollack

The pollack is almost exclusively a fish of rocky ground, where it is often caught by holiday anglers feathering, spinning or float fishing with sandeels or ragworms. Mostly these are smaller fish up to about 2lb or so, but much bigger pollack, sometimes approaching double figures, are caught every year. Targeting these bigger fish requires a bit more effort but the reward can be some of the most exciting shore fishing to be found in the Bay.

Think of a pollack as a mugger, an underwater hit-man, a fish whose feeding method is all about ambush, swallowing prey whole before it realises what is happening, and then think of

Pollack country
A fine lure-caught pollack from a rock mark on the Llŷn peninsula

the conditions that make successful muggings possible, and you will be thinking in the right direction. Many rocky areas, be they natural features or man-made breakwaters have points where the tide speeds up into a rip as it goes around them. In some places this may only happen on the flood or the ebb and you will need to do a bit of fieldwork to establish the pattern. Tidal rips are the killing grounds for larger predatory fish like pollack. Small baitfish like sandeels simply do not have the strength to fight a rip current and are swept along with it. A sandeel that finds itself in such a situation is tempting fate because down-tide, and alongside the rip, the predators are waiting in ambush. They will spot a baitfish coming through and charge up, engulfing it and immediately diving back into the quieter water to wait and watch again.

Both float and lure fishing serve to exploit this situation. In both cases the trick is to fool the pollack into assuming it is looking at a natural baitfish. This involves getting the depth correct, and with lures the speed of retrieval needs to be spot-on. Remember that the lure must resemble a baitfish being swept along by the tide, so that if its speed exceeds that of the current, or if it cuts strongly across or against the flow, it will tend to make a fish suspicious. In many cases the effective retrieval speed can be surprisingly slow, so be prepared to experiment and when you find a speed that produces results, stick to it.

Choice of lure is perhaps a bit less critical with pollack than it is for bass and I've had good pollack when feathering for mackerel on numerous occasions. However, to single out the better fish I tend to use largish sandeel imitations of around six to eight inches, such as the Slug-go or Red Gill, both proven catchers. These I rig leger-fashion with a three-ounce drilled bullet as the sinker, permitting reasonably long casting and allowing the lure to be fished deep if required. Large Dexter Wedges and small pirks are also productive, both giving good casting distance and having actions that lead to vicious takes.

A big pollack taking an interest in a lure tends to manifest

Pollack on the rocks
When the pollack are feeding hard, soft-lures like the Slug-go can produce good catches

itself by three or four taps followed by everything going solid, but at the same time bouncing, as the fish sets off on its first power dive. The dive must be controlled or it will take you into snags, which is why light lines are not my choice for this type of fishing – 20 to 30lb line gives you a chance. As the fish comes in, further dives can be expected, which, in areas where fleets of lobster pots and their buoys and ropes abound, likewise need to be controlled. Landing a large pollack can be tricky but is often facilitated by using the layout of the rock at the mark to advantage (finding useful shallow gullies, avoiding close-in snags and so on). This is one situation where I have found long rods most useful – they offer a distinct advantage in controlling things close in and steering the fish to your intended landing spot. If there is any swell, time landing the fish with an incoming wave, when the water will help lift the fish, rather than an outgoing one when the water will be cascading off the rocks, dragging the catch back downwards.

In late autumn and early winter, larger pollack can turn up in all sorts of places and will take large fish and squid baits. Mostly one-off catches in a session, these fish can nevertheless give you a surprise – like the one that took a mackerel bait I had deployed with conger in mind, one November night off the end of Holyhead Breakwater a couple of years back. It hit the bait so suddenly and with such force that I had to lunge for my rod, which was fast disappearing over the breakwater wall. I caught it by the butt-end, but it was a close thing. The culprit was, it turned out, just a five-pounder.

Coalfish

Coalfish (or coley) are a bit similar in appearance to pollack but the easy way to distinguish the two is to check the lateral line which runs along each flank. With pollack, this is dark whereas with coalfish it is pale, as shown in the identification images. Active predators with the same aggressive tendencies as pollack, it is a pity that larger coalfish are primarily an offshore species and on the Cardigan Bay shore one is more likely to meet with smaller specimens up to a couple of pounds. In the summer months, small coalfish are sometimes present in abundance on the deep water rock marks and around breakwaters, where strings of them are sometimes caught by anglers feathering for mackerel. In the winter months, they take up residence along some surf beaches, where they may be caught on worm and shellfish baits. These winter coalies are often better fish of a few pounds and can put up a good scrap, although nothing compared to the monsters that lurk on the mid-channel wrecks.

Ling

An inhabitant of the twilight world of deep water and jagged rock, the ling is unmistakable with its elongated, eel-like body and large mouth with a single barbel on the chin. They are caught most years on the deep water rock marks, especially during the winter months, taking fish baits like mackerel or pouting fillets primarily intended for conger. Inshore specimens tend to be small for the species with a double-figure one being an excellent result: like coalfish, the real rod-benders are an offshore proposition. Being active predators, they will also take lures, something I have experienced on rock marks on the west coast of Scotland when deep-spinning with artificial sandeels. At the time of year when ling are most frequently caught on the Cardigan Bay marks, most anglers are using bait and I wonder if a slowly-retrieved lure, fished deeply, might throw up a nice surprise?

Minor members of the Cod family

Pouting are found over a wide range of ground and are of a similar size to whiting, but deeper in the belly, sometimes with a couple of vertical dark stripes along their flanks. Like whiting, they will take most baits, but very few anglers would target them on purpose, except to use as bait for bass, conger eels and other predators. They have a poor eating reputation as their stomach juices quickly spoil the flesh after death – gutted immediately though, they are said to be quite good.

Poor cod are mostly too small to even contemplate eating and are caught mostly over rocky ground. They are not dissimilar in appearance at first encounter to small whiting, but the sure way to identify them is that their silvery scales come off readily when handled. Shedding scales is a defence mechanism adopted by many fish species – if a predator grabs at a poor-cod, it will sometimes be left with a mouthful of scales as the fish makes its quick getaway.

Tadpole-fish (also known as the greater forkbeard), are unusual looking, almost black all over – a species that entirely justifies its name. It is occasionally caught in rocky ground, where it can grow to a pound or more, and is more of a curiosity than anything else.

Rocklings (or 'slugs', as they are often referred to) are familiar to any angler who fishes a lot in winter. There are three species of these elongated fish. Firstly, and most frequently, the five-bearded rockling occurs over sandy and mixed ground and will attempt to eat any bait, no matter how big, especially if it involves lugworm. The 'beards' are whisker-like barbels – the five-bearded obviously having five around the mouth. Secondly, the shore rockling is often found over mixed to rocky ground. It is a drab brown colour, often with paler mottlings, with three barbels and rarely exceeding 12 inches in length. Thirdly, the three-bearded rockling is a more occasional catch from rough ground. It is a much fiercer-looking beast, a vivid pale orange with black leopard-spots all over, and often reaches 2lb or more. It has a large mouth and most specimens are taken at night on sizeable fish baits intended for conger eels.

EEL FAMILY – overview

The eel family enjoys a wide distribution with some 800 species known globally. However, there are only two species of these distinctive, elongate fish that anglers will meet with in Cardigan Bay – the European eel (more commonly called freshwater or silver eel) and its much larger cousin, the conger eel.

European eel

This wonder of biology has a bimodal fresh/saltwater existence. The young arrive in our inshore waters having drifted for many months in the currents of the Gulf Stream. Seeking fresh water, they make their way into estuaries and thereby into the river-systems, from where they take up residence in appropriate locations. These include rivers, ponds or ditches and I've even come across them when exploring old, flooded underground mine workings: the main prerequisite is a good supply of food. During the freshwater phase of their existence (7 to 20 years in males and 9 to 50 years in females) the fish is brownish with yellow flanks. Upon reaching sexual maturity, they take on a silvery colour, hence the alternative name.

Newly-arrived juvenile eels are tiny, clear and threadlike: known as glass eels or elvers, they used to be netted in great quantities. However, during the past few decades, catches have dramatically declined and in recent years the International Council for the Exploration of the Seas (ICES) has declared the European eel stocks to be outside of safe biological limits. In other words the fishery is unsustainable. Any specimens caught by anglers in freshwater or at sea must be returned to the water by law.

The onset of sexual maturity leads in turn to a remarkable spawning migration. On dark, damp nights they set off on the amazing journey that takes them across land, through river systems and estuaries and finally to the open sea. Here, they stop feeding and embark upon the final, 4000 mile stage –

crossing most of the Atlantic to the Sargasso Sea, between Bermuda and the Bahamas, where they spawn and then die. It is during the early part of this migration, before they have stopped feeding, that they are occasionally caught – most frequently in estuaries by anglers targeting flounders. Open beaches near river mouths will also produce a few. They take small strips of mackerel, worms and other baits, and are best known for leaving rigs in a tangled, slimy mess. They have small mouths, so larger baits do not lead to hook-ups. Given their protected status perhaps that is no bad thing.

Conger eel

Compared to the European Eel, congers have a more straightforward lifestyle. They spend all their time in the sea, lurking in dark nooks and crannies and seizing any prey unlucky enough to come too close to their hidey-holes. Congers are present all year round at deep water marks though in very cold weather they may vacate shallower waters, being rather sensitive to low temperatures. They grow to a large size – females can reach well over 100lb and the Welsh shore caught record is 40lb. Although this only sounds like a fraction of the maximum possible size, I can assure you that landing such a fish from a cramped rock ledge would be a major task that would severely test almost any rod and reel – and angler. Big congers are phenomenally powerful fish.

Fishing for congers is a matter of locating areas where they are likely to feed. This means rough ground like the piles of boulders that surround breakwaters and deeply fissured rocky shorelines. They are sometimes taken from mixed ground beaches too, especially in autumn and early winter when, following the shoals of pouting and whiting, they tend to wander around a bit.

A conger fishing session needs careful planning. They are relatively difficult to handle so you need to work out how you will land your catch before you start, picking an appropriate spot where you can get close to the water without slipping or getting caught by a swell. It is no good to simply start fishing in a carefree manner only to find an hour later that you have an angry 20-pounder thrashing about many feet below your stance – with no idea how to get down to it.

A well thought out approach extends to tackle too. A strong beachcaster matched with a robust multiplier reel loaded with 30 to 40lb line, and a leger rig incorporating a strong swivel, a single hook-length of 100lb or stronger mono and a large, strong 6/0 hook is the typical outfit. Rotten bottom rigs with makeshift sinkers get the bait down to where the eels are likely to be found. Take frozen or fresh mackerel and squid for bait but at the same time put a second rod out for pouting and poor cod. Both these species make up a lot of a conger's diet and a fresh pouting, or fillet from one, is particularly effective bait. Once the bait is cast out, put the reel in free spool and click on the reel's ratchet. Now the waiting game begins.

More congers are caught by night than by day, though daylight captures are possible in very deep water – especially with small specimens. A conger bite is often rather subtle – the ratchet making a series of short clicks. This is the time to act – if not, the fish will move off with the bait and get back to its sanctuary. Once there, no amount of pulling will shift it. Put the reel into gear, strike into the fish and lift like mad in one continuous motion. You will feel the eel backing-off, but give it all you have got to get it up in the water where if it does take a little line it can't get to a bolt-hole. Fight it out in mid-water, where the conger will often start spinning around like crazy, and let it tire before you land it.

Congers are eaten by some people but take some effort to dispatch. I once saw one that was apparently dead suddenly come to life and slither off seaward quickly. The best bet is to place the catch in a large frying oil-type bucket, where they won't be able to escape so easily. Personally I put the odd conger I catch back – there are better eating fish out there. Unhook using long-nosed pliers and a cloth to hold it firmly (they are especially slimy and writhe around powerfully) – and above all make sure it doesn't get the chance to bite you. Congers have sharp teeth and incredibly strong jaws. Handle them firmly but carefully and you will be less likely to have any problems.

FLATFISH FAMILY – overview

Flatfish are a familiar sight to anybody who has checked out a fishmonger's slab. They are unusual amongst the various orders of fish because in their youngest stage after hatching, they have the typical, symmetrical roundfish shape, living up in the water with the plankton. However, a metamorphosis then occurs, so that they end up with both eyes on one side of the head, a process involving either one eye or the other migrating around the head. This variation means that some flatfish species have their left side facing upward and some their right side. Either way, the process is for a very simple purpose: it prepares them effectively for a life spent on the seabed.

The flatfish clan is well represented in Cardigan Bay with, as far as anglers are concerned, three species widespread and five localised to rare. These are the flounder, dab and turbot, with the less-frequently met with, plaice, sole and topknot, the rare brill and the extremely rare halibut. All but the topknot have one thing in common – they dwell over sandy ground. However they have considerable differences in feeding habits, which in turn means that tactics have to be different. Of all of them, the flounder is probably the easiest to catch.

Flounder

Flounders used to be very common around the Cardigan Bay shoreline but in some areas numbers have sadly been reduced by trawling for lobster pot bait. They inhabit estuaries and have a wide tolerance to changes in water salinity. They are even caught in the lower reaches of freshwater rivers on occasion by sea-trout or salmon anglers fishing with worm baits. Estuarine fish make poor eating due to the muddy environment, but those that inhabit the cleaner sand around estuary mouths and the nearby surf beaches are much better. They run up to 2 to 3lbs in size but fish around a pound are more frequent. Brown to greenish-brown, they are a rather drab, mottled fish, with a white underside that can sometimes have pigmented areas. Sometimes they carry small orange spots on the back which can lead to them being mistaken for plaice, which have larger, scarlet spots.

Spawning offshore in the late winter, flounders are ravenous and therefore easy to catch in the spring, but these are spent fish with watery flesh that are not worth eating and are best left alone. By autumn, they are in much finer fettle, feeding hard ready for the next spawning migration. They readily take most baits, especially worms, crab and shellfish and when storms rip up the inshore sandbanks they will invade and feed along the surf beaches. Razor is excellent bait for them in such conditions. Leger or paternoster rigs with size 1 fine wire hooks are ideal and like many flatfish, flounders are attracted by 'bling' – beads and sequins and perhaps a small attractor spoon threaded onto the hook-length and stopped just above each hook. As flounders are attracted to movement, one effective method is to cast out and then periodically retrieve the rig, a few inches at a time.

Flounders can be caught by night or day and often feed in surprisingly shallow water, both off beaches and in estuaries – which makes them an ideal beginner's fish where casting skills are still under development. The best fishing is often around the outer sandbar complexes of estuaries, at night and in rough weather.

Dab

Dabs are small flatfish with pale golden-brown backs, sometimes flecked with orange and feeling rough to the touch.

Catching a dab over a pound in weight can certainly be regarded as a good result. Excellent eating fish, they are present all year round but the best fishing is in autumn and winter. Dabs do not seem to like rough conditions but good catches may be taken during flat calms at low water on shallow sandy beaches – night tides always being best. They seem to be aware that coming too close to the water's edge brings the risk of getting stranded and thus the best results are often to be had by long casting. Clean ground off deeper water rock marks can also produce them in good numbers though if you feel unhappy with fishing such areas at night, daytime can still produce a few. They also invade the outer parts of estuaries (if heavy rain and rivers in spate haven't filled them with fresh water) where they may be caught when fishing for flounders.

Dabs feed on small shellfish and other bottom dwelling creatures, but larger ones also eat small fish like sandeels and sprats. The best baits for them are worms and shellfish. Razor and black lugworm are usually reliable and easily obtained. Size 2 to 4 hooks are best as dabs have small mouths, and paternosters with short hook-lengths are typically used, though leger rigs are better if fishing off steep rocks into deeper water to make sure the bait stays on the seabed. They will also take mackerel strips, but as these are more likely to attract dogfish, it's best to stick to lugworms and razor, perhaps just using a sliver of fish to tip-off the bait.

Turbot

Apart from the halibut, the turbot is our biggest flatfish. Every year, boat anglers catch large, 20lb-plus specimens from sandbanks in the English Channel and elsewhere. Ashore, a five-pounder is regarded as an excellent catch, definitely warranting a celebratory pint. The Welsh shore caught record came from the beach south of Tywyn in 1984 and was an impressive fish of just over ten pounds. They are easy to identify – apart from their size, they have a speckled dark brown appearance and the skin on the back has many bony tubercles.

The turbot is a prized eating fish and has been targeted for years by commercial interests, so their numbers aren't what they were. They can still show up though over any sandy ground, with the shallow surf beaches offering the best chance. However, they move about a lot and as a consequence the better specimens may only be found over a few tides in their key seasons – spring and autumn. This I have found to be the case time after time. Anglers who do well with turbot tend to do so because they have put in a lot of time and dedication. The rest of the time it is juveniles that are mainly caught, together with a few pan-sized fish.

Turbot are masters of camouflage, merging imperceptibly into the background on a seabed composed of sand, fine gravel and shell debris. They use this to great advantage, pouncing on any passing smaller fish with speed and engulfing them whole with their huge mouths. Sandeels, whitebait, small flatfish, whiting and other small fish that inhabit sandy areas are their staple diet but they will also take crabs on occasion – as stomach contents of specimens I have caught have shown. But the mainly fishy diet indicates the correct approach – fish baits that can be presented in a reasonably lifelike manner.

Although sandeels do work, in my experience the best bait for turbot is a large piece cut from a mackerel fillet. Best of all is the tail section, cut 3 inches long and hooked just the once through the tough skin at the root of the tail. On a 2ft hook-length, such a bait will flutter about in the surf. A plain lead will let the rig move about a bit to add to the effect. Strong but small hooks (I use the Mustad Viking pattern, size 1) are unobtrusive and so complete the deception.

Surf conditions are critical, with a short onshore chop caused by the wind ideal. Rough seas and flat calms are generally a waste of time. Keep the casts short (30 to 50 yards) – you need to be fishing in the water tables as they push shoreward. They share this feeding zone with small-eyed

Turbot bait
The best bait is the tail section of a mackerel fillet, hooked through the very tough skin of the root, for short range casting into the surf tables

rays and flounders and at times the latter can peck the baits to bits. Longer casts outside of this range can still produce but will more likely find dogfish. Dull weather by day can yield results, but night tides are best of all, when other forms of disturbance are at a minimum.

Bites are typically a series of insistent tugs – very similar in fact to those of dogfish. On occasion, there will be numbers of small fish present, and the best way to avoid hooking undersized turbot is to up the bait size so that they are unable to engulf it – a five-pounder, given time, could swallow a whole mackerel without difficulty, so there is plenty of scope upwards. They hug the seabed as they are being brought in, feeling mostly like a dead weight, so sports fishermen need not apply.

Plaice

Although an important shore angling target around many parts of the UK coastline, in Cardigan Bay plaice tend to occur in rather localised populations and are a rather infrequent catch. Some of the sandy grounds of the south-west and north-west produce a few, both from open beaches and from rock ledges, with occasional good specimens being reported from the outer channels of the bigger estuaries too. Similar tactics to those used for dabs are effective, with plenty of 'bling' being commonly used. Worm and shellfish baits, often tipped with thin squid strips, are effective, but peeler crab is worth using in the summer months, especially in estuaries (if the school bass don't find the baits first, which they usually do). Unlike dabs, plaice are avid daytime feeders and tend to stop feeding once it is properly dark. Fairly settled weather improves the chances of success: rough conditions with coloured water offer poor prospects for this species.

Sole

Of the four members of the sole family of flatfish, the Dover sole is the only one of great interest to the rod-and-line angler. With the characteristic tongue-like shape that it shares with the other species, it is occasionally taken at night, from late summer into autumn, from shallow surf beaches using worm baits on small hooks legered hard to the seabed – though not in anything remotely like the numbers and sizes seen in some of the hotspots dotted around the English and Bristol Channel coasts. I've never heard of anglers setting out to specifically target them in Cardigan Bay. However, they do require a little more thought because they seem to require absolutely static baits. Specialists in fishing for sole often use a three-hook paternoster rig with short four inch hook-lengths and, most importantly, a weight at either end. Typically, a standard breakout-type sinker sits at the bottom of the rig to anchor it but at the top of the rig a drilled bullet is incorporated, thus ensuring that both ends of the rig are hard on the seabed where the sole can find the baits.

Rarer flatfish

The remaining three species are mentioned in passing as possible catches. Firstly, the brill. This is a similar fish in diet and habits to the turbot, but with a more oval appearance and lacking the bony tubercles on its back. I have never caught one, or heard of any catches, from the Cardigan Bay shore although they have certainly been landed by anglers on offshore charter boats on rare occasions. It seems, therefore, that they stay out in deeper water. They may thus be filed under 'possible but unlikely'. The topknot is unusual among the flatfish in that it inhabits rocky areas. It is a small fish that is best filed amongst the mini-species. Aberystwyth Stone Jetty, Fishguard breakwater and various rock marks have all produced occasional examples but it is not targeted on purpose. Some readers might well query why I list the third of these possible species, but the question of whether halibut are present in the Bay was answered a few years ago, at Pen-ychain near Pwllheli, when one of just under four pounds was caught by a 13-year-old boy on a sandeel bait, photographed and returned. On this basis, it is not unreasonable to wonder if there may be others out there. Speculation is always fun and gives anglers something to mull over when the fishing is a bit quiet!

MINOR PREDATORS

This bunch of mostly unrelated species (mackerel, garfish, scad, sea-trout, gurnards and weevers) have one thing in common in that they are all active predators, often shoaling up to attack whitebait and other fry. Some, like mackerel, are among the most commonly fished-for species in the bay, whilst others are primarily accidental by-catches: they are nevertheless included for the sake of completeness and (in the case of weevers) safety.

Mackerel

Every spring, large numbers of mackerel move up into Cardigan Bay in response to rising sea temperatures. Eaten fresh from the sea they have to be the most delicious fish in our waters.

They are also useful because having a stock in the freezer will ensure a handy bait supply for winter whiting and other species. The first of the year are usually caught from the deeper water of the Bay's extremities – in some years as early as mid-April. By midsummer, the deep water marks often have mackerel in abundance, but in the shallows that dominate the inner areas of the Bay, fairly settled weather is required for them to show up in numbers. Rough summers equate to poor mackerel catches over the shallower grounds. They will stay on through the autumn months, and in an Indian summer will be present in good numbers – the last ones departing at some point in November once sea temperatures start to drop.

Mackerel feed in two ways. In the winter months, they filter feed on plankton way offshore to the south-west of Wales. This, and more specifically, the gunge their stomachs contain as a consequence, may be the reason for the old wives' tale that mackerel eat sewage. I'm still told this one quite often, although an obvious debunking can be provided by pointing out that mackerel have been around for a lot longer than human civilisation and its sewer systems. But outside of this filter feeding period, mackerel are ferocious carnivores. Working mob-handed, baitfish (such as whitebait) are herded together into ever tighter shoals, thousands strong. The mackerel then charge open-mouthed through them, snapping up and swallowing as many fish as possible. The water surface may sometimes appear to boil when this is occurring. On beaches, they drive the prey to the water's edge, pinning it there, where some in their panic to escape may beach themselves. If, when walking on a beach, you notice that the water's edge is littered with dead and dying whitebait, it's a sure sign that a mackerel shoal has been on the rampage.

On occasions like this, the first indication that there is a feeding frenzy going on will often be a mass of frantic bird activity – with shearwaters also feeding on the baitfish and gannets majestically diving to take the mackerel with gulls mopping up the mess of dead and mangled whitebait left

behind on the sand. Follow the birds and you will not go far wrong. This applies as much ashore as it does afloat. At other times, the activity is all taking place deep down, with little sign at the surface of the mayhem going on beneath the waves. But on occasion, especially from deep water rock marks, the presence of large quantities of mackerel will bring in larger predators, from bass right through to dolphins. Watching a pod of dolphins herd the mackerel into 'bait balls' (just as the mackerel do to the whitebait), and then charge them is an incredible sight. I witnessed such a spectacle whilst putting together the final draught of this text. Amazingly, some anglers leaving the mark as I was arriving were complaining about the dolphins spoiling their fishing. In my view, other marine-dwellers have a much greater entitlement to mackerel than humans – after all, if we fail to catch, we can always grab a bag of chips on the way home whereas if they fail to catch then they may starve. And is not sitting in such beautiful surroundings and watching the natural world at work sufficient reward in itself?

Aftermath of a mackerel rampage
The calling card of a mass attack by mackerel: night falls over a beach littered with dead whitebait that have jumped clear of the water in their desperate attempts to escape

In any case, the dolphins finished their lunch after a few hours and, putting away the camera and picking up the rod, I soon had enough fish.

Mackerel in feeding mode will attack anything that moves, which is why they are most often caught by feathering. Simply cast a string of feathers with a 3 or 4oz sinker into the water and retrieve slowly. You'll soon find out if they are there. Cover as much of the water as possible (both laterally and in terms of depth) for they are one fish that can be found anywhere between surface and seabed. When you encounter them, it is not unusual to get one on every hook. If rock fishing, avoid buying feather rigs with too many hooks for this reason – four hooks is a sensible maximum to manage if you get a 'full house' whilst fishing from a ledge 15ft above the sea. Or, if it's all you can get, cut a 6-hook rig in half, tying on new swivels to the severed ends. Attempting to wind six large mackerel up through mid-air is an easy way to strip the gears of a fixed spool reel – especially a cheap one. They may move through quite quickly, so swiftly unhook and kill them and get the rig back out there. But only keep fishing until you have as many as you need. Some of the best mackerel marks involve a long and steep climb back to base, which means that many anglers predetermine how many mackerel they are going to catch by the weight they feel they can tote back up from the sea. Mackerel have a thin protective coating over their bodies which is damaged by handling – if they are handled and then thrown back, they will almost certainly die. When you have enough, stop fishing for them. It's as simple as that.

When mackerel are abundant along popular sections of coast problems can arise due to the sheer numbers of once-a-year anglers going after them – with crossed lines, inappropriate casting, snapped-off rigs flying through the air, beer getting consumed to excess and tempers sometimes being lost. My advice is to avoid such situations. Find somewhere quieter – anywhere that requires a bit of a walk will always prove to be relatively peaceful. Or get up early and head down to the sea at first light. Dawn, as well as dusk, is a prime time for these fish. One of my favourite marks involves a twenty minute walk then a steep rock climb. Rarely have I ever seen anybody else there. Even popular beaches tend to be deserted at first light, when you will have miles of sandy shoreline to yourself.

Mackerel also take spinners (metallic colours are best) and can be caught by float fishing with small fish strips that they mistake for fry. One handy trick when they are scattered is to fish for other species with a leger or paternoster rig, above which is fixed an extra 3ft hook-length with a floating bead and size 6 hook baited with a small strip of fish. This will float up in the water and any passing mackerel will attack it.

Garfish

Like a marlin in miniature, the garfish is a long, slender fish with an elongated beak-like mouth. They are not uncommon inshore, arriving in spring and staying for the summer and early autumn months, but in contrast to mackerel, relatively few are caught. They are tasty but the unusual, bright green bones put some people off. Garfish can be caught from any type of venue, but are most frequently targeted from rock ledges, jetties and breakwaters. They will take small spinners, retrieved quickly so that they splash chaotically across the surface, and even feathers on occasion, but as the beak is bony, solid hook-ups can be tricky. The most effective technique is float fishing. Set the float to fish the bait 3ft below the surface, bait a size 6 hook with a strip of mackerel belly flesh (about the size of a small sandeel) and cast out. Feed the area in which you are fishing with a bit of groundbait, such as moistened bran mixed with pulverised or minced mackerel flesh, from time to time. Garfish respond well to groundbaiting. If there are no takes, increase the depth of the bait at increments down to about 10ft. However, generally speaking, you can expect to find them feeding fairly close to the surface. Quite often, the first indication that you have hooked a garfish will be to see one leaping out of the water repeatedly around your float. The floating beads rig, as described under mackerel, will also take this species.

Scad

The scad, or horse-mackerel, is occasionally caught from the shore on feathers when they are running with mackerel shoals. In addition, some are also caught on small fish-baits. They are not a dissimilar shape to mackerel, but they have a distinctive, hard keel of large scales running down the mid-flank on either side and particularly long pectoral fins. They are very bony, which puts some people off eating them, but they are certainly not inedible. A far commoner catch offshore, they are not usually targeted as such by shore anglers.

Sea-trout

Sea-trout, or sewin as they are called in Wales, are a voracious predator when at sea, and are occasionally caught on spinners or even on legered fish strips. It is important to note that you need a 'Migratory Fish' license from the Environment Agency to deliberately fish for them from the shore – and if you don't have one any caught by accident must by law be returned.

Gurnards

Five species of the gurnard family are met with in UK waters: the red, the grey, the tub, the streaked and the long-finned gurnard. Generally these are small fish although tubs grow to a fair size (when they make good eating) but such specimens are more likely to be caught offshore by boat anglers. The grey gurnard is a grey-brown mottled fish with a prominent dark spot on its dorsal fin, as shown by the identification image. The red gurnard is a bright scarlet colour. The tub gurnard can be mistaken for the grey, but it has no dorsal spot and the pectoral fins have a distinctive, bright turquoise-blue outer fringe. The long-finned gurnard is extremely rare; however, the streaked gurnard has been recorded off NW Wales: one was caught in 2012 by an angler fishing from a Holyhead-based charter-boat and having seen a photograph, the author went back through his collection of images to discover that he, unknowingly at the time, caught one amongst a haul of greys and reds from an Anglesey rock-mark in 2009! They look very much like red gurnards at a glance: the big difference being in the shape of the head, which is noticeably blunt, dropping steeply from the eyes down to the mouth, unlike the rather longer concave 'snouts' of the others. All gurnards have large pectoral fins, partly modified to form a series of 'feelers' either side of the rather squared-off head. As with all fish eaters, they have a disproportionately large mouth for swallowing prey.

Gurnards are summer fish. They live in moderate depths of water over sand, where they hunt for sandeels and other small fish. Beaches, shallow reefs, rocks and breakwaters giving access to clean ground will produce them, occasionally in numbers, though the usual pattern will be an occasional one in a mixed bag of fish. They take small strips of mackerel and squid and will often preferentially attack a moving bait. They are sometimes caught on mackerel feathers fished deep and even spinners.

Weevers

Two species of weevers, the greater and the lesser, are common in Cardigan Bay. Both are fish-eaters and boat anglers often catch greater weevers whilst feathering for mackerel. They are elongated, wedge-shaped fish with a body that tapers sharply down towards the tail. Greater weevers have darker diagonal stripes along their flanks while the lesser weever is more silvery, with pale brown mottling. Herein lies the danger – at a casual glance, lesser weevers look a bit like small whiting to the inexperienced. The danger is because these are two of the only three venomous fish in UK waters (the third being the stingray) and getting stung by one is a potentially serious and certainly painful experience. The illustrations show the essential features and are well worth studying carefully.

The venom in both species is delivered the same way. Spines on the black, sail-like dorsal fin and on either gill cover have, at their bases, venom-sacs which pump the poison into the victim, who has perhaps stepped on one whilst bathing or is handling one having caught it. The symptoms are a severe stinging pain and swelling of the affected area. The venom is protein-based and unstable to heat. Coastguards treat stings by immersing the affected area in piping hot water (not scalding hot, obviously). However, although most people make a good recovery, there have been cases of severe allergic reactions or other complications arising from the sting due to the patient having a pre-existing health problem. A weever sting should therefore be taken seriously in all cases and treatment sought immediately.

Lesser weevers are an inshore fish of sandy shallows and estuaries. For example, they are commonly caught off the jetty in Aberdyfi where Gwynedd Council has erected a notice (as it has in other popular beach venues), illustrating the fish and warning of the risk. They take small fish and squid strips on small hooks trotted along the sandy bottom. They are usually shaken off the hook but do not shake too aggressively as the fish might flip over and spike you! Some anglers unhook them with two pairs of long-handled artery forceps – one to hold the fish firmly, the other to remove the hook. The good news is that anglers using larger baits for more worthwhile food species are much less likely to encounter lesser weevers which are only a few inches in length. Greater weevers, on the other hand, grow to 18 inches or more and are aggressive hunters, hence their being caught on mackerel feathers at times. Catches from the shore though are relatively rare. They make good eating, but need to be dealt with very carefully, as even when dead they can still sting.

THE BARNACLE MUNCHERS

A general principle of marine biology is that no matter what type of ecosystem one looks at, a food-chain will have evolved that involves its regular inhabitants. Just like the regulars at a pub, each will be indulging itself in its own time-honoured way. Take steep, kelp-covered rocks, for example. Barnacles cover the rock surfaces, filter-feeding on the plankton carried along in suspension in the water. Limpets and periwinkles potter about almost imperceptibly as they graze upon algal films and the surfaces of kelp fronds and stems. And taking advantage of these potential but tough, thick-shelled food sources are two groups of fish that have evolved to cope with them: the wrasse and triggerfish families. Between them, they include many of the brightly-coloured fish that inhabit the world's coral reefs and the main thing they have in common in terms of physiology is that they are equipped with strong jaws and chisel-like teeth, equal to the task demanded of them. Some other families of fish share these physical features, such as the blennies, but in Cardigan Bay the blenny family is limited to a few various mini-species. Their big brother, the wolf-fish, with its fearsome dentition, is primarily a fish of northern and eastern UK waters.

Triggerfish

One species from this family, the grey triggerfish, is found in Cardigan Bay. It is a warm water species that has been extending its range northwards. A grey-brown fish with a very deep, flattened body and tough, leathery skin, a few examples are caught in most years from the shore and especially from boats in various parts of the Bay. Late in the year, sudden cold snaps can result in quite a few dead or dying triggers washing up along the beaches, suggesting that they are more widespread than angling catches would indicate. They show a strong preference for deeply gullied and creviced rock as this gives them both food and cover. Triggers have a useful defence mechanism in that the first dorsal fin consists of strong spines, one of which can be erected and then locked into place by the second (hence the name). By erecting and locking the spines, they can very effectively jam themselves into a crevice, where neither storms nor predators can get at them.

The same fishing methods as described for wrasse will suffice for triggers. They will take most baits if in feeding mood, with squid strips and crab particularly effective. Cardigan Bay does not have recognised shore hotspots for triggerfish (unlike the Bristol Channel where they are commonly targeted and caught off Mumbles Pier near Swansea). That said, anywhere with rough ground and a reasonable depth of water could potentially produce them during the summer and autumn months.

Wrasse

In Cardigan Bay, five species of wrasse are to be found – the ballan, cuckoo, corkwing, rock-cook and goldsinny. Of these, the ballan and corkwing are the most frequently encountered. All of the wrasse are rough-ground fish, found around reefs, deep water rock ledges and breakwaters. Although caught all year round in very deep water (except in the coldest winters), they are primarily regarded as summer fish, caught on those beautiful still warm days that have been uncommon in recent years, with the sea a clear crystal blue and the lack of swell making it possible to fish right at the water's edge.

Ballan wrasse grow to a fair size in Cardigan Bay's coastal waters – fish of 5lb are caught every year. Shallow reefs and breakwaters tend to produce smaller examples up to a couple of pounds or so but for the larger specimens you need to be fishing in deep water rock country. They vary an awful lot in appearance – red, orange, green and khaki are all combined into a spectacular range of mottled patterns, the larger specimens often being particularly impressive. Given their staple diet, it is one of angling's curiosities that they are especially partial to the least likely thing to be found in their habitat – lugworms.

Wrasse will attack lugworm baits like piranhas. Ragworm also works, but not as well, and for the bigger specimens crab baits are often used – not just peeler or soft crabs but hardbacks too. However, I have found frozen black lugworm to be perfectly effective, which means I can just grab some from the freezer or call at a tackle shop on my way to a mark.

In terms of rigs, either a sliding float rig or a single hook paternoster with a makeshift sinker is simple and straightforward, minimising snagging. A 30lb hook-length defeats their teeth, and a sharp size 1 to 1/0 medium-gauge hook (such as the Viking pattern) is ideal. The bite from a big ballan wrasse is a ferocious, lunging pull, quite capable of dragging an unattended rod into the sea, so pay attention! They are powerful fish that can give you quite a run around, although that first power-dive is always the strongest. Long-nosed pliers or artery forceps are useful for unhooking in order to keep fingertips away from those barnacle-crunching teeth. Ballan wrasse are edible and in France they are considered an important ingredient in bouillabaisse, but they are not commonly eaten over here.

The cuckoo wrasse tends to be confined to deeper water. It is easy to identify, especially the male, which has a vivid blue head and outer tail, with an orange flank but with further blue lines – without doubt the most colourful UK sea fish. It will take a wide range of baits, including mackerel and squid strips. The other three wrasse encountered in Cardigan Bay are much smaller fish, regarded by many anglers as mini-species. The rock-cook and corkwing are a rather similar mottled olive and brown with red and blue lines near the mouth, but the rock-cook has a darker brown band around the base of the tail and a much smaller mouth in proportion to the body size (another name for it is 'small-mouthed wrasse'). The goldsinny is a plain golden colour with a black spot at the front of the dorsal fin and another on the upper base of the tail.

MINI-SPECIES

The term 'mini-species' refers to a wide range of smaller fish that are mostly caught by accident. By this I mean that they are typically caught when fishing into rough ground from breakwaters using small hooks and baits such as ragworm, by anglers not targeting any one species as such but instead seeing what might be about. Although small, some have surprisingly large mouths and appetites, so that size 1 hooks baited with mackerel strips for other species can often result in sea-scorpions being caught. Blennies and gobies are also a frequent catch over rough ground and off breakwaters, while dragonets occur over sandier ground. None of these species are venomous. Some, like the sea-scorpions and dragonets, have sharp backward-pointing spines around the head and gill-covers. To avoid getting spiked, use a cloth to hold them while unhooking and, above all, learn to distinguish them from the distinctive-looking weevers, which are dangerous, using the images provided

MULLET

Three species of true mullet occur in Cardigan Bay's coastal waters – the thick-lipped, the thin-lipped and the golden grey. Another fish, the red mullet, is unrelated except by its common name. Of the true mullet species, the thick-lipped is the most common. A large, solid silvery fish that can reach over 10lb in weight, it shoals in harbours and in estuaries, but also feeds in the open sea. The thin-lipped mullet is primarily an estuary fish, whilst the golden-grey prefers shallow sandy surf beaches. All are fish that are primarily targeted in the warmer months.

Mullet fishing is one of the most specialised branches of sea angling and many books have been written on the subject. There is a National Mullet Club, with a website and publications where you can get the best advice from the regulars who fish for these elusive species (almost exclusively in some cases).

Only a brief summary is offered here, as few anglers using standard beach gear and baits will catch one. The reasons for that will become apparent when you read further.

For the thick-lipped and thin-lipped varieties, coarse fishing tackle is used – a match-rod, light lines of well under 10lb breaking strain, small but strong size 8 to 10 hooks and small floats. Bread is the most used bait, but in some areas maggots or even sweetcorn are popular. Whatever the bait used, groundbaiting, either on the day, or leading up to it in order to get the fish feeding on what you are using, is very important. Maggots can work well when a big tide starts to break up heaps of rotting seaweed, releasing the grubs of seaweed flies into the water. Some anglers have even successfully developed tactics to catch them by fly fishing.

When not otherwise persuaded, mullet feed normally on algae and protozoans which they obtain by scraping along the surface of the mud found in estuary channels. These scrape marks can often be seen at low tide. When they are feeding, they are out of sight, and a common mistake is to assume that the big shoals often seen swimming about high in the water will be easy to catch. Far from it – these fish are simply basking in the sunshine, whilst the gunge they have been feeding on is digesting in their specialised gut.

Golden-grey mullet have localised populations along central Cardigan Bay's beaches, where they are sometimes caught by anglers fishing small ragworms (or bunches of harbour ragworms) on small size 6 hooks. Flounders and school bass accompany them so such tactics tend to lead to a mixed catch if conditions are favourable. They are easily identified by the golden patch on each gill-cover.

The red mullet may be mentioned in passing. It belongs to the goatfish family and is distinctive in appearance, being red-orange in colour with large, carp-like scales and a blunt head with two long whiskery appendages sticking out from the chin, which it uses to detect food. The diet is worms, small crustaceans and shellfish and most of the occasional captures that I am aware of have been on worm baits fished hard on the seabed. Commercial catches elsewhere in the southern UK suggest that this species may be extending its range northwards and if so then perhaps more of these tasty fish will be putting in an appearance in the coming years.

RAY FAMILY – overview

Rays are one of the most successful of the various groups of fish, having been around in some form or other since the Jurassic Period. They are all slow-growing fish, some of which get to a large size – the so-called common (it isn't any more) skate gets to over 200lb. All have similar features – a flat, diamond to disc-shaped body, dark above, white below, with a long tail extending out behind, a mouth with powerful crushing plates (as opposed to teeth) on the underside and eyes atop. Rays feed primarily on things that they find or catch on the seabed, which is why most are caught on legered baits. They swim powerfully by flapping their 'wings' which are in fact drastically modified pectoral fins. It is the wings that one sees on fishmongers' slabs. However, since the numbers of rays are declining, I would strongly recommend that any that you catch are returned.

Eight species of ray are likely through to just about possible captures along the Cardigan Bay shore. Other species might just conceivably turn up on rare occasions, but would be regarded as very unusual. Thirty years ago, and for many years previously, the mainstay catch of the Cardigan Bay charter boat fleet was the abundant thornback ray, but heavy commercial exploitation has decimated them. Today, they are just an occasional catch from boat or shore, mainly during the spring and autumn months. Small-eyed rays may be caught along shallow surf beaches, arriving in spring and remaining inshore until late autumn, although they sometimes move off for a bit during the midsummer months if conditions are not to their liking. Spotted rays are sometimes caught in

Mouth of a ray
The mouth of a ray is equipped with bony plates capable of grasping and crushing prey. Thus, it can feed on soft-bodied and shelled food items

late winter through to early summer from sandy patches in mixed ground. Cuckoo rays are a rare turn-up from similar terrain. Undulate and blonde rays would both be very notable, newsworthy catches. The eighth species, the stingray, is a rare and potentially dangerous summer catch.

The best baits vary a little from species to species, but the overall approach is similar. Use a leger rig with a hook-length of at least 25lbs breaking strain (and from rock marks 40lbs gives that added margin of safety), with medium to fairly heavy-gauge hooks in size 1 to 4/0 depending on the species and size of bait. Use pliers to remove the hook – those bony plates can crush fingers. To avoid getting cut by the thorns that some species have, hold the fish in a damp cloth as you carry it back out into a reasonable depth of water so that it can swim off safely.

Thornback ray

Thornbacks generally like a fair depth of water over them, though in calmer conditions they may hunt in the shallows. Identification is easy – they have bony nodules complete with sharp thorns (just like those on the stem of a rose bush), all over their backs. Colour varies a little although mottled browns are typical. They have a varied diet of crabs and other crustaceans, small fish and shellfish, though most captures come to oily fish baits like mackerel. Crab baits also account for a few, especially in the spring. The majority of thornbacks are caught at night, mostly from rocks that drop onto clean ground, but also from the shallower sandy beaches. I have caught occasional specimens from shallow venues whilst fishing for turbot in the early autumn. A 10lb thornback is a good one these days, although much bigger specimens would be possible if there was less commercial pressure. The Welsh record is a fish of over 31lb, caught from a boat off north Wales over 30 years ago.

Small-eyed (or painted) ray

This ray has no thorns and its back is a pale tan-brown with a series of off-white lines on either wing. It has a far more spectacularly marked cousin, the undulate ray, but that is primarily a fish of the English Channel. However, if you catch a ray that, compared to the images provided in this book, looks like it was designed by someone heavily into psychedelia, do get its identity checked by taking a digital photograph for a marine biologist to examine. Returning to fish that you are likely to catch, small-eyed rays feed primarily on sandeels and other small fish and more are taken on that bait than any other, although mackerel comes a close second. However, like most fish they are opportunists, so that squid baits will not be ignored and I've even had the occasional one on lugworm. They feed in surprisingly shallow water at times, where they will yank the rod butt off the ground as they move off after engulfing your bait. An energetic fish as rays go, they will often make short runs through the surf parallel to the beach prior to being landed. Fish to 10lb or more are again possible though this is generally a smaller species.

Spotted ray

Spotted rays are tan-brown in colour, having an evenly-spaced pattern of small, rounded dark brown spots with a group forming a single circular marking on each wing. The larger and much rarer blonde ray also has a spotted appearance but lacks the circular feature. Spotted rays are caught primarily on sandeel or crab baits. They rarely exceed 2-3lb in weight. Rocks with sand patches or mixtures of stony weed beds and finer gravel, in a medium depth of water, are their preferred hunting ground. The Gimlet Rock area of Pwllheli Beach is a mark that has yielded a fair number over the years, but any similar ground around the Bay could produce. Very occasionally, the cuckoo ray (another small species with a similar lifestyle) is caught from similar terrain and on similar baits. They have a plain, pale tan-brown upper side but with a conspicuous large black and creamy-yellow mottled spot in the middle of each wing.

Stingray

An early summer visitor to the Bay, the stingray is the largest of the ray family that the shore angler is likely to encounter. The Welsh shore caught record was landed at Fairbourne in Gwynedd in 1991 and was a monster of 54lb. Compared to the other ray species, the stingray is noticeably thick-bodied with a medium to dark olive-brown back and a thin whip-like tail. The tail carries the sting – a barbed bony venomous dagger-like feature that can cause a nasty puncture wound and which often breaks off in the flesh. Urgent medical attention is without doubt required in the event of a sting.

They take worm, crab and sometimes fish baits. Being powerfully built, they are quite capable of dragging a rod into the sea and landing one can be quite a struggle. In the unlikely event of catching one, handle it with great care and, all-importantly, keep out of range of that tail, which is surprisingly mobile – like the whip of a scorpion. Stingrays love warmth and will purposely seek out inshore shallows in order to bask in the sunshine. Warm, settled spells of weather from late May through to August seem to see the most captures. Such shallow waters are especially widespread in the north-eastern corner of the Bay and the Pwllheli district has, in particular, seen a number of specimens caught in recent years. Despite that, they are not frequent catches and many regular Cardigan Bay shore anglers have yet to see one in the flesh.

SHARK FAMILY – overview

The shark family is one of long lineage – their ancestors are some of the earliest fishes in the fossil record, having been around for over 400 million years. In Cardigan Bay, ten species are encountered. One, the huge basking shark, is a plankton eater occasionally seen cruising along from rock marks, but is more commonly observed from boats. Of the other bigger species, the fish-eating blue and porbeagle sharks are mostly encountered offshore, though the porbeagle has occasionally been seen very close to land when the mackerel are inshore in large numbers. The tope, a close relative to, but smaller than the blue shark, is caught from the shore on occasion. Monkfish (or angel shark) have very occasionally been taken from the central Cardigan Bay coast. Of the smaller species, the bull huss is a dogfish that can reach over 10lbs in weight and is a regular catch over rough ground. Its much smaller cousin, the lesser spotted dogfish, can show up pretty much anywhere, often in huge numbers. Spurdogs used to be caught in early winter from deep water marks but commercial pressure has made it very uncommon. Conversely, the smooth-hounds which are crab and mollusc crunching sharks with bony plates instead of teeth, have healthier, albeit localised populations in some mixed ground areas.

Tope

This sleek and powerful predator sometimes comes within casting range at some deep water marks that give the angler access to mixed or clean ground. Some of the deeper beaches also produce them from time to time and in settled conditions they could in theory show up just about anywhere, often giving their presence away by biting off baited hooks. Although large mackerel baits are commonly used for tope, the main reason why these fish visit the inshore waters is to hunt down flatfish such as flounders and dabs. Experienced tope anglers cottoned on to this long ago, with good results recorded using baits fashioned from fillets taken from these flatties.

Tope can grow to well over 50lbs and have a classic, textbook shark appearance including a large mouth bristling with razor sharp teeth. The skin is grey and very rough to the touch as it is covered with sharp dermal denticles. Anyone wanting to try and catch one needs to keep all that armour in mind. A steel wire or very heavy monofilament trace with a strong sharp 6/0 to 8/0 hook crimped to it (these are available ready-made in tackle shops) is essential. A heavy shock leader prevents the dermal denticles from chafing through the main line should they come into contact with it. When boat fishing, a so-called 'rubbing leader' is used for exactly the same purpose. The only reel up to the job is a multiplier – when a tope takes a bait it often charges off at a rate of knots, taking several tens of yards of line with it. The reel needs to have the drag set fairly loose so that the fish can take line, or your rod will go flying into the sea. Multipliers have a ratchet that will buzz when the reel spool is turning so the standard practice is to engage this as it will wake up an angler about to nod off when a fish takes. There are two schools of thought with respect to timing here – some anglers hit the hook home at the first run, others let the tope pause, turn and gulp down the bait a bit before it starts its second run and then strike. I'm with the former school – you might miss the odd fish but what you won't ever get is one that has swallowed the hook, with the damage that does.

Attention needs to be paid to the drag on the reel when bringing a tope in – it needs to be able to take line under pressure, or further runs or lunges could pop your main line. Once within reach, the tail and dorsal fins offer a firm grip. Unhook using long-nosed pliers or a long T-bar, keeping fingers well away from those teeth. Tope are relatively inedible (unless you like the taste of ammonia) and should always be released to keep stocks healthy. They are regarded by people who don't primarily fish for food as sport fish and many specialists use barbless hooks for them. As I fish for my supper on the whole, I don't tend to target them, although I have caught a few small ones on shallow surf beaches in late summer and bigger specimens whilst boat fishing.

Monkfish

Looking like a cross between a ray and a shark, the monkfish is unmistakeable with its flattened body and large, tooth filled mouth on the underside of the head. The Welsh shore caught record of 52lbs was caught at Llwyngwril, between Tywyn and Barmouth, in 1984, but none have been reported more recently. It has been suggested that they disappeared at the same time as the thornback rays were decimated by netting, in the early 1990s. However, there have been occasional reports in recent years from certain central Cardigan Bay surf beaches, involving heavy, slow-moving but 'unstoppable' fish being encountered. Monkfish? Who knows, for in each case the fish was not even seen, but there are very few candidate species that could produce this behaviour.

That said, owing to its rarity the monkfish was awarded protected status in 2008, which makes it illegal to even target them, either on a commercial or recreational basis. Likewise any incidental landings must be returned to the sea straight away, but do take a quick photograph and report any such catch to the Shark Trust. Just to confuse matters, the completely unrelated anglerfish, a large, underwater mugger with a huge upward pointing toothy mouth for engulfing prey and an extremely unlikely shore catch hereabouts is commercially sold as 'monkfish'.

Bull huss

Huss are worth targeting from early spring right through to late autumn. Brown to very dark brown with large blackish spots, they have a seriously rough hide that can easily graze unprotected human skin. They also have sharp teeth, much smaller than those of tope but able to give a nasty nip to the careless nevertheless. As well as mackerel or pouting fillets, they will readily take sandeels and they are partial to frozen squid. Hook-lengths of 100lb mono will not only be huss-proof but will also handle the much toothier conger eels that often inhabit the same ground. Huss don't run hard as a rule but will repeatedly tug in a determined way at the rod tip. Quite commonly, they grasp the bait between their teeth, swim happily in with it as you reel in then spit it out at the last minute, thereby having the last laugh. For those that are actually hooked, unhooking requires long-nosed pliers. They are quite edible but the fillets need to be skinned first, which can be quite a job requiring pliers to pull the skin back and a sharp knife to pare the skin away. Another method is to steep the fillets in boiling water, when the skin comes away more easily in bits. Many anglers put them back, preferring to eat more easily dealt with species.

Lesser-spotted dogfish

Commonly referred to as the 'doggie', the 'woofer' or the 'LSD', this species is typically met with at around 1 to 2lbs in weight. Although similar in appearance to the huss its spots are smaller and its background colour is paler, typically being a sandy brown. This fish is the ultimate scent hunter, able

Jaws junior
Like most sharks, the lesser spotted dogfish has a good array of sharp teeth and widely-spaced nostrils to home in on the scent of food from afar

to home in on a strip of mackerel from way down tide. Fish baits attract them quickest but they will take anything that they come across. They can travel in large packs at times, when the rod tip will start nodding within seconds of casting out and the dogfish come in two at a time. This can be frustrating when targeting better eating fish and anglers are on occasion driven to despair by them. However, in such circumstances a handy trick is to move a few tens of yards downtide and you should be clear of them for a while, as then the ones you have moved away from will no longer be able to detect the scent of your bait. This has worked for me on many occasions. But you have to hand it to them – they are the product of millions of years of evolution and as bait sniffers they reign supreme. That said, one trait that dogfish do have is to become disorientated upon release, often swimming landwards and beaching themselves. Wade out a bit before slipping them back and keep an eye out for any that have become stranded. After they've been taken back out once or twice they'll figure things out and head off out to sea. Just be careful when handling them as, like huss, they have a sandpaper hide and they are very adept at wrapping their tails around a bare forearm and then writhing about, leaving the skin red and sore. Grab them by head and tail simultaneously, then bring the hand holding the tail around so that you can also grasp the head with it and that option is closed to them. Now that your other hand is free the fish can be quickly unhooked using long-nosed pliers. As for edibility, some anglers enjoy eating them but the same preparatory steps are required as for huss.

Spurdog

The spurdog is the tastiest of our inshore sharks and as a consequence it is now a very infrequent catch from the shore. Only twenty-five years ago vast packs of spurs would sweep through offshore Cardigan Bay every year, some making their way closer in. Sadly, long-liners from elsewhere moved in and hammered and hammered them on an industrial scale to the point of near wipe-out, so that catching them from boat or shore has become nothing more than a memory. Every Cardigan Bay sea angler of long experience will recall this appalling travesty.

Spurs, as they are often called, are grey, classic shark shaped fish whose dorsal fins both carry sharp spines that can cause a nasty wound for the unwary. They range from dogfish sized up to 10lb or more. My memory banks tell me that they are easily skinned and I've always suspected that the origin of the term 'rock salmon' (that is today applied vaguely to all dogfish) originated from this pink fleshed species. Deep water rock marks and breakwaters used to produce a few to fish-baits, although the catches by anglers were a tiny fraction of the thousands of tonnes that were taken by the long-liners. Their teeth are small but sharp, so that strong traces of 50lb mono are necessary even for small specimens. If this species makes a comeback and starts showing again from the rock marks, please release any that happen to be caught, giving the stocks the best possible chance to recover. We must start to learn by our mistakes.

Smoothhounds

Two varieties of smoothhound are found in the Bay: the Common and the Starry. The Starry normally has white spots along its flanks although this is not an absolute rule and when spotless it can be difficult to distinguish from the Common. Both have a classic shark shape, but instead of teeth they have crushing plates similar to those of rays. This gives the game away with respect to diet – these fish go about crunching things with hard shells, which is why the majority are caught on legered crab baits intended for bass. When one takes such a bait, it will shoot off with a similar energy level to a tope, but being smaller it will be a bit easier to control once the angler has recovered from the surprise. Knowledgeable local anglers target them during the summer months and are justifiably reserved about broadcasting exact details of the marks, but in general, mixed ground, with plenty of crab-friendly territory – boulders, weed and so on, is where they may be expected. Most catches are of relatively small examples and a double-figure smoothhound would be an excellent specimen from the Cardigan Bay shore. They are edible but so are dogfish. Enough said.

AN HISTORICAL NOTE

This is by no means an exhaustive list of the fish you could, potentially, catch in the waters of Cardigan Bay, though it covers what you will catch 99.9% of the time and several of the species listed would make news if you were to catch them.

For a complete listing (and a fascinating snapshot of local marine ecology over a century ago), *A Handbook to the Vertebrate Fauna of North Wales*, by H. Edward Forrest, published in 1912, makes for some interesting reading. Amongst the rarer species, Forrest lists the comber (a sea-perch – *Serranus cabrilla*) as 'rarely on the west coast'; the dentex (*Dentex dentex*) as having been recorded near Pwllheli, the John Dory (*Zeus faber*) as 'occasionally taken off the west coast' and the wolf-fish (*Anarrhicus lupus*) as having been 'recorded off the west coast and in Menai Straits'. Of the red sea-bream (*Pagellus bogaraveo*) it notes, 'Mr. S. G. Cummings says Sea Bream are very abundant off Anglesey wherever the coast is rocky and water deep: he used to catch many with rod and line off outlying rocks in autumn'. Of haddock, it is stated that 'the years 1894-8 were marked by an abundance of Haddock off the Dee estuary', whilst of halibut, 'Dr. J. F. Lister has taken one or two small ones off Barmouth'.

Other flatfish listed include 'fairly common' brill, long rough dab (*Hippoglossus vulgaris*) from the Menai Straits, occasional megrim (*Lepidorhombus whiffiagonis*), fairly common lemon sole (*Microstomus kitt*) and the solenette (*Buglossidium luteum*) being 'one of the most abundant of indigenous fishes in the shallow waters of the Dee estuary'. The presence of the streaked gurnard off the coast of Anglesey had not gone unnoticed back then although it was described as 'rare'. In all, some 130 species of marine fish are listed: perhaps the saddest entry of all is the following:

'COMMON OR BLUE SKATE. *Raia batis*. L. Plentiful.'

This species is now regarded by many as effectively extinct in the Irish Sea, and endangered in other areas.

If, having gone through the following images, you can't identify what you've caught, but have a photo on your camera or mobile, then why not join one of the online sea-angling forums (a search using that as the key will find them quickly), and post the image there? You will generally find that help will be swiftly to hand and if a rare species it will generate a lot of interest.

For a more in-depth look at the identification and ecology of sea fish, *The Sea Angler's Fishes* by Michael Kennedy is indispensable. (If your public library can't help you, Coch-y-Bonddu Books – www.anglebooks.com – always has second-hand copies in stock).

Bass
(not sea-bass,
just bass)

Latin name:	*Dicentrarchus labrax*
Description:	Elongate fish with bright silver flanks and darker backs (black on bigger specimens); large scales. Distinctive, upright spiny dorsal fin and sharp bony plates on gill-covers.
Distribution:	Throughout inshore Cardigan Bay.
Preferred habitat:	Wherever there is food - bass can be found along surf beaches, in estuaries, over reefs and on mixed ground.
Seasons:	Bass are caught all year round but late March–late November sees the majority of catches.
Food:	Opportunist feeders that will take whatever is available in season.
Eating:	Highly regarded. Minimum size: 37.5cm (although the WFSA recommends 45cm).
Welsh shore record:	7.600kg/16lb 12oz (Aberthaw, 1980).

Black bream

Latin name:	*Spondyliosoma cantharus*
Description:	A deep-bodied, large-scaled fish, silvery with a purplish tint and sometimes with vertical darker bars along its flanks.
Distribution:	Localised populations in northern and central sections of the Bay.
Preferred habitat:	Mixed ground and shallow, pebbly reefs with eelgrass.
Seasons:	Black bream appear in late spring and are usually gone by mid-autumn.
Food:	Varied diet that includes various marine organisms but also red coralline seaweeds.
Eating:	A tasty fish. Minimum size: 23cm.
Welsh shore record:	2.070kg/4lb 9oz. (Pwllheli, 2003).

Codling

Latin name:	*Gadus mohua*
Description:	Big-headed, broad-shouldered, rather pot-bellied especially in larger specimens; white underside and mottled brown flanks.
Distribution:	Scattered around the Bay with localised populations resident around reefs.
Preferred habitat:	Mixed to rough ground and along beaches with such ground nearby, especially after storms.
Seasons:	Sometimes caught in summer over rough ground but mostly an autumn-winter species.
Food:	Cod are opportunist feeders, taking anything that is available.
Eating:	Good. Minimum size: 35cm.
Welsh shore record:	20.185kg/44lb 8oz (Barry Island, 1966). In Cardigan Bay a ten-pounder would be a superb catch.

Haddock

Latin name:	*Melanogrammus aeglefinus*
Description:	Classic cod family shape but the first dorsal fin is noticeably long. Brown back, white underside and dark lateral line with a diagnostic dark 'thumb mark' straddling it above and behind the pectoral fin base.
Distribution:	A not infrequent catch to the charter fleet that works the deeper offshore grounds off SW Wales towards the Celtic Deep: an unlikely but not impossible catch from the deepest rock marks accessing clean ground in the far NW and SW of Cardigan Bay.
Preferred habitat:	Clean ground and deep water.
Seasons:	Late spring–late autumn.
Food:	Crustaceans, worms and molluscs.
Eating:	Edible but owing to its local rarity any catches should be returned.
Welsh shore record:	0.482kg/1lb 1oz (Watwick Steps, Pembrokeshire, 1994).

Whiting

Latin name:	*Merlangius merlangus*
Description:	Silvery-white with a pale brown, sometimes slightly black-flecked back and a golden-brown lateral line. Small but very sharp teeth.
Distribution:	Very widespread throughout Cardigan Bay.
Preferred habitat:	Mostly over sandy ground.
Seasons:	Larger fish invading inshore waters en masse in autumn and leaving again in late winter; juveniles present all year round.
Food:	Other fish, dead or alive, and worms, crustaceans, shellfish.
Eating:	Good. Minimum size: 27cm.
Welsh shore record:	1.62kg/3lb 9oz (Cold Knap, Barry, 1994).

Pollack

Latin name:	*Pollachius pollachius*
Description:	Broad-shouldered, muscular fish, greenish-brown back, bronzed or golden flanks. Lateral line dark brown.
Distribution:	Widespread around Cardigan Bay wherever its preferred habitat exists.
Preferred habitat:	The rougher the better – rocky coasts, manmade structures, fast tide rips.
Seasons:	Present all year round in deeper water, most frequent late spring to late autumn.
Food:	Active predator that will take any other fish it can engulf; will take other foods such as crustaceans.
Eating:	Good. Minimum size: 30cm (WFSA recommend 36cm).
Welsh shore record:	6.57kg/14lb 8oz (St David's, Pembroke, 1999).

Coalfish

Latin name:	*Pollachius virens*
Description:	Black back, silver lower flanks, white lateral line.
Distribution:	Throughout Cardigan Bay with concentrations in both the NW and SW extremities.
Preferred habitat:	Rough ground with strong tides but will come into surf beaches at times.
Seasons:	From deeper water marks, all year round, but late autumn and winter along the surf beaches.
Food:	Small fish, crustaceans, shellfish.
Eating:	Good. Minimum size: 35cm.
Welsh shore record:	3.232kg/7lb 2oz. (Sker Rocks, South Wales, 1994).

Pouting

Latin name:	*Trisopterus luscus*
Description:	A rather deep-bodied fish with noticeable large eyes. Bronze-coloured to grey-brown, sometimes with a couple of vertical darker stripes on the flanks.
Distribution:	Widespread in Cardigan Bay.
Preferred habitat:	Rocky ground, either natural or manmade; mixed-ground beaches. less frequently over sandy areas.
Seasons:	All year round in deeper water areas, but most frequent in autumn and early winter.
Food:	Fish, worms, small crustaceans, shellfish.
Eating:	Poor reputation but said to be good if gutted promptly after capture. Minimum size: 20cm (WFSA).
Welsh shore record:	1.22kg/2lb 11oz (Port Talbot, 1980).

Poor-cod

Latin name:	*Trisopterus minutus*
Description:	A small fish, less deep-bodied than pouting and with a golden to pinkish brown back. Sheds scales very readily when handled.
Distribution:	Throughout Cardigan Bay.
Preferred habitat:	Commonly found over rough to mixed ground and around manmade structures.
Seasons:	Most commonly caught in summer and autumn.
Food:	Both fish and worm-baits taken, suggesting it has wide-ranging tastes and is opportunistic.
Eating:	Too small to consider eating. Minimum size: 16cm (WFSA).
Welsh shore record:	305g/10.8oz (Holyhead, 1982).

Tadpole-fish

Photo: Carl & Pam Worrall

Latin name:	*Raniceps raninus*
Description:	Unmistakable charcoal-grey fish with a large head and mouth out of all proportion to the rest of the body.
Distribution:	Widespread but in small numbers.
Preferred habitat:	Primarily found in rocky country.
Seasons:	Occasional reported catches all year around.
Food:	Fish and crustaceans – hence the large mouth, but will take a wide range of baits.
Eating:	Generally too small to consider eating. Minimum size: 18cm (WFSA).
Welsh shore record:	510g/1lb 2oz (Fishguard, 1976).

Ling

Photo: Gethyn Owen

Latin name:	*Molva molva*
Description:	Elongated fish, mottled pale brown back and flanks, white underside and one large barbel under chin.
Distribution:	Localised to its preferred habitat and rarely seen elsewhere.
Preferred habitat:	Deep water with a rocky seabed, occasionally from man-made structures where the depth is sufficient.
Seasons:	All year round with shore catches very infrequent but predominantly during the winter months.
Food:	Other fish – catches are generally made by anglers fishing for the more abundant conger eels.
Eating:	Good. Minimum size: 63cm.
Welsh shore record:	4.08kg/9lb (Barry, 1984).

Five-bearded rockling

Latin name:	*Ciliata mustela*
Description:	Elongated small fish with brown to grey-brown back. Large mouth for its size, four barbels above mouth and one on the chin.
Distribution:	Widespread around Cardigan Bay.
Preferred habitat:	Sandy to rocky ground.
Seasons:	'Slugs', as they are dispassionately called, invade the beaches of Cardigan Bay in late autumn and winter.
Food:	Anything it can find and often caught on surprisingly large baits.
Eating:	Generally too small to consider. Minimum size: 16cm (WFSA).
Welsh shore record:	480g/1lb 1oz (Aberystwyth, 1995).

Shore rockling

Latin name:	*Gaidropsarus mediterraneus*
Description:	Elongate fish, deep brown to pale brown, plain or sometimes with paler mottled pattern (but not spotted like the three-bearded rockling). Three barbels around large mouth, two above and one below.
Distribution:	Widespread in Cardigan Bay's inshore waters.
Preferred habitat:	Primarily a fish of rough ground, like its three-bearded big brother.
Seasons:	All year round.
Food:	Will eat any food items it can manage.
Eating:	Generally too small to consider. Minimum size: 20cm (WFSA).
Welsh shore record:	467g/1lb 0.5oz (Aberfraw, Anglesey, 2004).

Three-bearded rockling

Latin name:	*Gaidropsarus vulgaris*
Description:	Elongated orange-brown fish with distinctive, darker-brown 'leopard-spots'. A large mouth with three barbels on head, two above mouth and one below.
Distribution:	Widespread wherever preferred habitat is to be found.
Preferred habitat:	Rough ground, shallow to deep, both natural and around manmade structures.
Seasons:	Present all year round but most frequently caught after dark in autumn, winter and spring.
Food:	Fish and crustaceans – it may engulf large baits intended for conger eels.
Eating:	Good. Minimum size: 23cm (WFSA).
Welsh shore record:	1.27kg/2lb 13oz (Anglesey, 1985).

Freshwater eel

Latin name:	*Anguilla anguilla*
Description:	Grey to greenish-brown eel, greenish flanks. Sexually mature fish heading off to the Sargasso Sea to spawn take on a silvery-white appearance. The lower jaw protrudes a little and the dorsal fin begins well behind the pectoral fins, distinguishing it from the conger.
Distribution:	Widespread but numbers have fallen dramatically in recent years.
Preferred habitat:	A fish that divides its time between freshwater rivers and lakes and the sea where it is met with inshore, especially in estuaries and harbours where it is occasionally caught by anglers fishing for flounders.
Seasons:	All year round.
Food:	Will eat anything edible that it comes across.
Eating:	The freshwater eel is a threatened species and all catches must be returned by law.
Welsh shore record:	Vacant.

Conger eel

This was caught at Trefor, just around the corner from Cardigan Bay!

Photo: Karen Hancox

Latin name:	*Conger conger*
Description:	Unmistakable large eel with powerful body and large mouth equipped with sharp, grasping teeth. The dorsal fin starts ahead of the pectoral fins, which helps distinguish small specimens from freshwater eels.
Distribution:	Throughout Cardigan Bay wherever the right habitats are present.
Preferred habitat:	Rough, rocky ground, mixed ground and occasionally along beaches adjacent to same.
Seasons:	All year round in deeper water but they tend to abandon shallower areas in colder winters.
Food:	Ambush-predator that eats various other fish, plus crustaceans and octopi/squid.
Eating:	Edible but an acquired taste! Minimum size: 61cm (WFSA).
Welsh shore record:	18.144kg/40lbs. (Port Talbot, 1996).

Flounder

Latin name:	*Platichthys flesus*
Description:	Drab, mottled in shades of brown, occasionally greenish-brown; some have orange spots but much less vivid than those of the plaice. Creamy white underside.
Distribution:	Throughout inshore Cardigan Bay's shallower areas.
Preferred habitat:	Over sandy to muddy substrates, in estuaries and along beaches.
Seasons:	Smaller fish all year round; larger fish typically March-January (outside of spawning time), best fishing October–January.
Food:	Crustaceans, shellfish, worms, small fish.
Eating:	Flounders from the open sea are tastier than those from tidal rivers. Minimum size: 25cm.
Welsh shore record:	1.772kg/3lb 14.5oz. (St Ishmaels, Pembroke, 2000).

Dab

Latin name:	*Limanda limanda*
Description:	A small flatfish, pale brown to golden brown with 'spots' consisting of small orange flecks. Scales on back feel rough to the touch.
Distribution:	Throughout Cardigan Bay
Preferred habitat:	Sandy substrates inshore, offshore and in outer parts of estuaries.
Seasons:	All year round but with a marked increase in autumn and winter.
Food:	Worms, small crustaceans, shellfish, small fish.
Eating:	Very good. Minimum size: 15cm (WFSA 23cm).
Welsh shore record:	1.162kg/2lb 9oz. (Port Talbot, 1936).

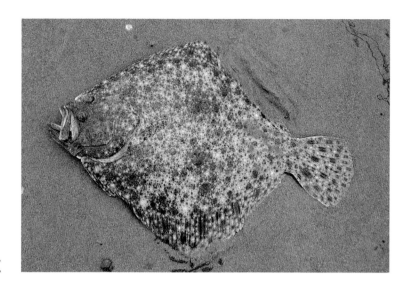

Turbot

Latin name:	*Scophthalmus maximus*
Description:	Diamond-shaped flatfish with a well-mottled back in shades of brown, covered with bony wart-like tubercles. Large mouth.
Distribution:	Throughout the Bay.
Preferred habitat:	Over sand, fine gravel, shell-gravel.
Seasons:	April–June and September–November for larger specimens; juveniles present all year round.
Food:	Primarily uses ambush tactics for fish that it can swallow whole; also crustaceans.
Eating:	Highly-regarded. Minimum size: 30cm
Welsh shore record:	4.649kg/10lb (Tywyn, 1984).

Plaice

Latin name:	*Pleuronectes platessa*
Description:	A brown-backed flatfish with vivid scarlet-orange spots. Juveniles also have pale flecks as in the above specimen. The skin feels smooth to the touch but the head has bony tubercles.
Distribution:	Scattered around the Bay although populations seem localised with this species uncommon from the shore in some areas.
Preferred habitat:	Over sandy, sometimes muddy ground including some estuaries, often near to pea-mussel beds.
Seasons:	Spring–autumn with most frequent catches in late spring and early summer.
Food:	Shellfish, small crustaceans, worms, small fish such as sand-eels sometimes.
Eating:	Very good. Minimum size: 27cm.
Welsh shore record:	3.2kg/7lb 1oz (Deganwy, 1983).

Dover sole

Photo: Gareth Davies

Latin name:	*Solea solea*
Description:	Distinctive, tongue-shaped flatfish with a pale to mid-brown back, white underside and small mouth.
Distribution:	Localised but does occur in Cardigan Bay.
Preferred habitat:	Over sand, mud, shell-gravel.
Seasons:	Summer into early autumn.
Food:	Small worms and crustaceans.
Eating:	Highly-regarded. Minimum size: 24cm
Welsh shore record:	1.899kg/4lb 3oz (Barry, South Wales, 1991).

Topknot

Latin name:	*Zeugopterus punctatus*
Description:	Rather oval in shape, perhaps almost rectangular, with rough scales on the dark to mid-brown back and a disproportionately small tail, but the dead giveaway is the habitat.
Distribution:	Around Cardigan Bay most of the rather infrequent captures have been from breakwaters.
Preferred habitat:	Inshore waters and exclusively over rocky ground – it clings to underwater rock surfaces with its body.
Seasons:	Caught in the warmer months along with other mini-species.
Food:	Small fish, crustaceans.
Eating:	Too small to be regarded as edible.
Welsh shore record:	0.14kg/5oz (Fishguard, 1996).

Atlantic halibut

Photo: Chris & Adam Doyle

Latin name:	*Hippoglossus hippoglossus*
Description:	Large flatfish, relatively narrow with a noticeably forked tail (unique to UK flatfish) and large mouth.
Distribution:	Little data with respect to Welsh waters but does occur in Cardigan Bay, as evidenced by the photos! Another specimen weighing 8lb plus was caught in the Bristol Channel in 2002 on a charter boat.
Preferred habitat:	Over sand, mud, shell-gravel.
Seasons:	This one was caught in the summer months.
Food:	Active predator taking other fish.
Eating:	Important commercially in other areas of the North Atlantic.
Welsh shore record:	At 1.73kg/3lb 13oz this specimen, caught between Criccieth and Pwllheli, would have done the job!

Mackerel

Latin name:	*Scomber scombrus*
Description:	A streamlined fish with a green back with thick black lines and an iridescent silvery flank. Large eyes and mouth.
Distribution:	Widespread: abundant some years, scattered during others, depending on conditions.
Preferred habitat:	A fish of the open sea, irrespective of type of seabed; may enter the outer parts of the bigger estuaries.
Seasons:	Spring–late autumn.
Food:	In winter, it tends to strain out plankton, but the rest of the time it is a voracious predator that works in shoals to herd and attack baitfish.
Eating:	Excellent when very fresh. Minimum size: 20cm.
Welsh shore record:	1.953kg/4lb 4.89oz (Porth Dafarch, Anglesey, 1990).

Garfish

Latin name:	*Belone belone*
Description:	Unmistakable due to the long, marlin-like bill. Elongated and silvery but with greenish scales.
Distribution:	Throughout Cardigan Bay.
Preferred habitat:	Where the baitfish go, the garfish will follow, being an upper water feeder.
Seasons:	Spring through to autumn.
Food:	Small fish such as sandeels or whitebait.
Eating:	Garfish are tasty despite the bright green bones. Minimum size: 31cm (WFSA).
Welsh shore record:	907g/2lbs (Anglesey, 1977).

Scad

Photo: Gareth Pickard

Latin name:	*Trachurus trachurus*
Description:	Streamlined fish with lateral 'keel' of large, hard scales forming a ridgelike feature. Pectoral fins are proportionately very long. Large eyes and upward-pointing mouth.
Distribution:	Widespread around Cardigan Bay in moderate numbers, especially offshore. Less frequent inshore.
Preferred habitat:	An open water swimmer that hunts over a variety of ground-types, especially reefs.
Seasons:	Summer and autumn.
Food:	An active predator that feeds on smaller fish, occasionally caught on lures intended for mackerel.
Eating:	Edible though very bony. Minimum size: 15cm (WFSA 23cm).
Welsh shore record:	907g/2lbs (Stackpole, Pembroke, 1998).

Sea-trout

Photo: Paul Morgan

Latin name:	*Salmo trutta trutta*
Description:	Elongate, powerfully-built fish with silver flanks, brighter underbelly and slightly darker back. Dark spots or blotches on back and extending a little below the straight lateral line.
Distribution:	Throughout Cardigan Bay.
Preferred habitat:	An inshore fish, congregating especially in the vicinity of river mouths.
Seasons:	Sea-trout breed in rivers, the young fish (smolts) heading to sea when around 20cm in length. They feed heavily in the sea, returning to the rivers in summer and autumn, and back again to sea after spawning. Bait anglers are most likely to catch recovering kelts in late winter and spring. By law they may only be taken between 1st May and 17th October, and only if one has an E.A. licence.
Food:	An active predator.
Eating:	Excellent – but note seasons above. Minimum size: 23cm (Environment Agency), but 30cm recommended.
Welsh shore record:	None listed by WFSA. UK (BRFC) record 12.850 kg/28lb 5oz. (Hampshire 1992).

Grey gurnard

Latin name:	*Eutrigla gurnardus*
Description:	Typical gurnard shape with disproportionately large head and mouth; large pectoral fins partially modified into 'feelers'; back and flanks mottled grey-brown to brown and the dorsal fin has a conspicuous dark spot.
Distribution:	Widespread in Cardigan Bay although commonest offshore.
Preferred habitat:	Clean, sandy ground, especially systems of sandbanks and gullies.
Seasons:	Late spring to mid-autumn.
Food:	Active predator that takes small fish and crustaceans such as shrimps.
Eating:	Good eating if large enough. Minimum size: 18cm (WFSA).
Welsh shore record:	453g/1lb (Port Dafarch, Anglesey, 1987).

Red gurnard

Latin name:	*Chelidonichthys cuculus*
Description:	Typical gurnard shape with disproportionately large head and mouth; large pectoral fins partially modified into 'feelers'; back and sides bright scarlet-red.
Distribution:	Widespread in Cardigan Bay although commonest offshore.
Preferred habitat:	Clean, sandy ground, especially systems of sandbanks and gullies.
Seasons:	Late spring to mid-autumn.
Food:	Active predator that takes small fish and crustaceans such as shrimps.
Eating:	Good eating if large enough. Minimum size: 25cm (WFSA).
Welsh shore record:	624g/1lb 6oz (Ty Croes, Anglesey, 1986).

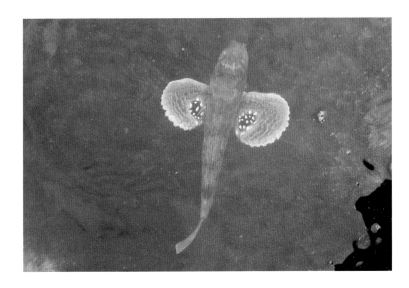

Tub gurnard

Latin name:	*Chelidonichthys lucernus*
Description:	The largest of the UK gurnards, it has a typical gurnard shape with disproportionately large head and mouth and large pectoral fins partially modified into 'feelers'. Brownish to orange-brown back and flanks, the distinguishing feature is the bright electric-blue rim around each pectoral fin. The fish in the image was released into a rock-pool filling up with the incoming tide, so that this colour-display could be seen to advantage.
Distribution:	Widespread in Cardigan Bay although commonest offshore.
Preferred habitat:	Clean, sandy ground, especially systems of sandbanks and gullies, and near to reefs, the margins of which they often hunt along.
Seasons:	Late spring to mid-autumn.
Food:	Active predator that takes small fish and crustaceans such as shrimps.
Eating:	Good eating if large enough. Minimum size: 25cm (WFSA).
Welsh shore record:	5.528kg/12lb 3oz (Langland Bay, Gower, 1976).

Streaked gurnard

Photo: Gethyn Owen

Latin name:	*Trigloporus lastoviza*
Description:	Very similar to other gurnards, especially the red, but a much blunter head. Unlike the others, where the snout is more elongated and deeply concave from the eyes to the mouth, this gurnard has a steep 'forehead' that is only slightly concave. Typically red but the large pectoral fins may have electric blue markings. The skin along the flanks has transverse ridges that originate at the lateral line.
Distribution:	May be more widespread than previously thought, although regarded as a rare fish. Easily mis-identified – the author missed one at the time among a 2009 catch of red and grey gurnards, only noticing it later in one of his photographs from the day.
Preferred habitat:	Over clean ground and in a moderate depth of water.
Seasons:	As with other gurnards, primarily the warmer months of the year.
Food:	Small fish and crustaceans.
Eating:	Owing to its rarity, it should always be returned.
Welsh shore record:	Not listed by WFSA - the author could have claimed it!

Greater weever

Photo: Ian Pratt

Latin name:	*Trachinus draco*
Description:	An elongated brownish fish with a large upturned mouth and a pattern of diagonal stripes along each flank. Fins may be fringed with blue. The black sail-like dorsal fin is connected to venom sacs, as is the single clear spine on each gill-cover and either can deliver an excruciatingly painful sting requiring medical attention.
Distribution:	Widespread through Cardigan Bay, especially offshore. Uncommon from the shore.
Preferred habitat:	Caught over a variety of grounds, especially of a sandy to stony nature.
Seasons:	Spring to autumn.
Food:	Ambush-predator that lies almost buried in the sand waiting to pounce on unsuspecting passing small fish or shrimps – often caught when feathering for mackerel.
Eating:	Good, but extreme care must be taken when handling them. The safest technique is to kill the fish then cut away and discard (back into the sea) the head and dorsal fin by a diagonal cut requiring a very sharp knife, thereby removing both sources of danger. A good pair of barbecue tongs is often used to keep things from slipping. Long-handled artery forceps help in unhooking. Minimum size: 25cm (WFSA).
Welsh shore record:	440g/15.5oz (Aberystwyth, 2005).

Lesser weever

Latin name:	*Echiichthys vipera*
Description:	Small silvery-yellow fish with upward-pointing mouth that at a glance may be mistaken for other species such as small whiting. Careful! The black sail-like dorsal fin is connected to venom sacs, as is the single clear spine on each gill-cover and either can deliver an excruciatingly painful sting requiring medical attention.
Distribution:	Widespread around inshore areas of Cardigan Bay.
Preferred habitat:	Shallow, sandy waters including beaches and outer estuaries where it may be extremely common.
Seasons:	Spring through to autumn.
Food:	Ambush-predator that lies almost buried in the sand waiting to pounce on unsuspecting passing small fish or shrimps.
Eating:	A mini-species, not regarded as a food fish.
Welsh shore record:	80g/2.32oz (Pendine, Carmarthen, 1989).

Triggerfish

Latin name:	*Balistes capriscus*
Description:	A very deep-bodied fish, almost like a flattened disc, with tough thick skin, large scales and greyish to brownish back and flanks. Substantial set of incisor teeth. The first dorsal spine is very strong and is connected with the second spine so that the latter can solidly lock the former into place when erected and conversely release it - the 'trigger' mechanism. This it uses to jam itself safely into underwater hidey-holes.
Distribution:	Widespread in Cardigan Bay but individual populations tend to be very localised.
Preferred habitat:	Rough ground in shallow to moderate depths of water: likes deeply gullied rock where it can take up residence.
Seasons:	Mid-summer through to late autumn: an early cold snap can see individuals washing ashore having succumbed to the cold.
Food:	Shellfish and crustaceans.
Eating:	Good but must be skinned first according to those who eat them. Minimum size: 25cm (WFSA).
Welsh shore record:	2.154kg/4lb 12oz (Mumbles, 1992).

Ballan wrasse

Latin name:	*Labrus bergylta*
Description:	A thick-set, powerful fish and by far the largest of the UK wrasse. Large scales, powerful paddle-like fins and rabbit-like teeth for chomping barnacles and other hard food. Colour highly variable: juveniles are often rather drab in shades of green and brown whilst mature fish can vary from scarlet to orange to golden to green, sometimes with white spots. Two examples illustrated.
Distribution:	Throughout Cardigan Bay wherever its preferred habitat is available.
Preferred habitat:	Rough ground without exception, from shallow reefs to deep water undersea rock-faces.
Seasons:	Present all year round in deeper areas but in all situations most likely to be met with from May– November.
Food:	Barnacles, crabs, shellfish like mussels, worms, occasionally small fish. Often caught on lugworm baits - which do not occur in its natural habitat!
Eating:	Regarded by most as inedible. Minimum size: 31cm (WFSA).
Welsh shore record:	2.948kg/6lb 8oz (Freshwater West, Pembroke, 1977).

Ballan wrasse

Cuckoo
wrasse

male and female

Photos: Kevin Doughty and
Gethyn Owen

Latin name:	*Labrus mixtus*
Description:	The second biggest wrasse in UK waters and much more elongated in appearance than the Ballan; males and females so different in colour that they were once regarded as different species! Male red to orange with blue to electric-blue markings along the body and about the head. Females golden to pinkish-yellow with much fainter, pale blue-grey markings.
Distribution:	Widespread through Cardigan Bay wherever the preferred habitat occurs.
Preferred habitat:	Rough ground without exception but very rarely found in shallow areas: hence this fish is far more commonly caught by boat anglers.
Seasons:	Almost all catches are during the summer months.
Food:	Crustaceans, shellfish, small fish, worms.
Eating:	Regarded as inedible by most anglers. Minimum size 18cm: (WFSA).
Welsh shore record:	680g/1lb 8oz (St Davids, Pembroke, 1986).

Cuckoo wrasse

male and female

Corkwing wrasse
male and female

Latin name:	*Symphodus (Crenilabrus) melops*
Description:	A small wrasse that again varies strongly in colour between males and females: the male has bright blue markings on a brown to red-orange background whereas the female has similar patterns but entirely in shades of brown, occasionally with a bit of green mixed in.
Distribution:	Widespread in Cardigan Bay especially inshore.
Preferred habitat:	Rough to mixed ground, shallow to deep. Common around manmade structures.
Seasons:	Spring through to the first cold weather of winter.
Food:	Shellfish, crustaceans; those that live around jetties get used to a wide-ranging diet.
Eating:	A mini-species, not regarded as a food fish.
Welsh shore record:	290g/10.2oz (Menai Straits, 1995).

Corkwing wrasse

male and female

Rock-cook wrasse
(also known as Smallmouth wrasse)

Latin name:	*Centrolabrus exoletus*
Description:	Distinguished from the corkwing by having flanks of a more uniform golden to orange colour, the blue markings confined to around the much smaller mouth. The root of the tail typically has a vertical dark brown bar.
Distribution:	Localised populations are found around Cardigan Bay.
Preferred habitat:	Rough ground with plenty of shelter and a reasonable depth of water: deepwater breakwaters see the most catches.
Seasons:	Typically a fish of the summer months.
Food:	Small crustaceans, worms and molluscs.
Eating:	A mini-species, not regarded as a food fish.
Welsh shore record:	75g/2.65oz (Holyhead, 1981).

Goldsinny wrasse

Latin name:	*Ctenolabrus rupestris*
Description:	A small and somewhat elongate wrasse, golden colour and with two prominent dark spots, one near the start of the dorsal fin, the other at the top of the root of the tail.
Distribution:	Localised populations are found around Cardigan Bay.
Preferred habitat:	Rough ground with plenty of shelter and a reasonable depth of water: deepwater breakwaters see the most catches.
Seasons:	Summer into autumn.
Food:	Small crustaceans, worms and molluscs.
Eating:	A mini-species, not regarded as a food fish.
Welsh shore record:	102g/3.6oz (Menai Straits, 1995).

Black goby

Latin name:	*Gobius niger*
Description:	A small pot-bellied dark brown fish, with large dark brown to black blotches along each flank; pop-eyed with a sail-like first dorsal fin which is clear, barred with brown.
Distribution:	Apparently widespread but rarely caught owing to its small size.
Preferred habitat:	Mixed to rough ground; around breakwaters and piers.
Seasons:	Present all year round.
Food:	Small fish, crustaceans and worms.
Eating:	A mini-species, not regarded as a food fish.
Welsh shore record:	58g/2oz (Pembroke Dock, 1981).

Rock goby

Latin name:	*Gobius paganellus*
Description:	A golden-brown goby with mottled flanks. The first dorsal fin has a pale golden band along the top.
Distribution:	Apparently widespread but rarely caught owing to its small size.
Preferred habitat:	Mixed to rough ground; around breakwaters and piers.
Seasons:	Present all year round.
Food:	Small fish, crustaceans and worms.
Eating:	A mini-species, not regarded as a food fish.
Welsh shore record:	35g/1.23oz (Caernarfon, 1993).

Leopard-spotted goby

Photo: Gareth Pickard

Latin name:	*Thorogobius ephippiatus*
Description:	This is the easiest of the gobies to identify, with its pale flanks and orange to brown blotches.
Distribution:	Apparently widespread but rarely caught owing to its small size.
Preferred habitat:	Rough ground with a reasonable depth of water.
Seasons:	Tends to be caught in the warmer half of the year, along with many other mini-species.
Food:	Small crustaceans, worms, fry.
Eating:	A mini-species, not regarded as a food fish.
Welsh shore record:	Not listed by WFSA.

Long-spined sea scorpion

Latin name:	*Taurulus bubalis*
Description:	A small fish with a distinctive proportionately huge head furnishing several spines, those on the sides being long and readily erected. Large mouth for size of fish with a small white lappet (barbel-like flap of skin) at each corner. Greenish to golden-brown; mottled; fins spotted.
Distribution:	Widespread through Cardigan Bay.
Preferred habitat:	Mixed to rough ground where there is useful cover to lie in wait for prey.
Seasons:	All year round.
Food:	Anything it can manage to swallow. Shrimps, prawns and small fish all taken.
Eating:	A mini-species, not regarded as a food fish.
Welsh shore record:	212g/7.48oz (Mumbles, 1992).

Short-spined sea scorpion

Latin name:	*Myoxocephalus scorpius*
Description:	A larger sea-scorpion: again variably coloured but the spines do not reach beyond the gill-covers and lacks the white lappets of the long-spined.
Distribution:	Widespread although not abundant.
Preferred habitat:	Rough to mixed ground with plenty of cover for ambush purposes.
Seasons:	All year round.
Food:	Anything it can manage to swallow. Shrimps, prawns and small fish (including other sea-scorpions) all taken.
Eating:	Not regarded as a food species. Minimum size: 23cm (WFSA).
Welsh shore record:	453g/1lb (Menai Straits, 1998).

Shanny

Latin name:	*Lipophrys pholis*
Description:	A small, mottled brown to dark brown fish with a large head and mouth armed with large sharp rabbit-like teeth.
Distribution:	Widespread through inshore Cardigan Bay.
Preferred habitat:	Rough ground–rocky shores and around manmade structures.
Seasons:	All year around, and especially common late spring–late autumn.
Food:	Small crustaceans and shellfish.
Eating:	A mini-species, not regarded as a food fish.
Welsh shore record:	170g/6oz (Holyhead, 1972).

Tompot blenny

Latin name:	*Parablennius gattorugine*
Description:	A small mottled brown fish with indistinct vertical barring; fins more orange-brown especially towards margins. Two orange-brown hornlike lappets over the eyes.
Distribution:	Widespread through inshore Cardigan Bay.
Preferred habitat:	Rough ground - rocky shores and around manmade structures, with a liking for deeper water than the related shanny.
Seasons:	All year around, and especially common late spring–late autumn.
Food:	Small crustaceans and shellfish.
Eating:	A mini-species, not regarded as a food fish.
Welsh shore record:	140g/5.94oz (Fishguard, 2000).

Dragonet

Latin name:	*Callionymus lyra*
Description:	Elongate mottled brown fish with large pectoral fins a bit reminiscent of those of gurnards. Long dorsal fin. Head armed with sharp spines that protrude beyond gill-covers and can give a nasty spiking to the careless! This is a female: the males can have blue colouration on the head and along the flanks.
Distribution:	Widespread but individual populations seem localised in nature.
Preferred habitat:	Over sand, often in fairly deep water.
Seasons:	Summer and autumn.
Food:	Small fry, worms, crustaceans.
Eating:	A mini-species, not regarded as a food fish.
Welsh shore record:	170g/6oz (Milford Haven, 2001).

Sand-smelt

Latin name:	*Atherina (Hepsetia) presbyter*
Description:	A small, mirror-bright fish with a dark green back. Large scales.
Distribution:	Widespread in inshore areas with localised population centres.
Preferred habitat:	Estuaries and harbours; sandy to mixed ground but often found quite high in the water.
Seasons:	Late spring to mid-autumn.
Food:	Small crustaceans, fry, worms.
Eating:	Used to be regarded as a delicacy: said to have a flavour reminiscent of cucumber.
Welsh shore record:	38g/1.34oz (Aberystwyth, 1994).

Herring

Latin name:	*Clupea harengus*
Description:	Bright silvery fish with iridescent blue-green back; large scales that readily detach; upward-pointed mouth and proportionately large eyes.
Distribution:	Widespread in Cardigan Bay.
Preferred habitat:	A fish of the middle and upper waters, over a variety of ground-types.
Seasons:	All year round but can be common in the autumn and winter.
Food:	Zooplankton; mature fish will eat smaller fish like small sand-eels.
Eating:	Excellent, but those caught from the shore are often small. Minimum size: 20cm.
Welsh shore record:	Vacant as of January 2012.

**Greater
sandeel
or Launce**
(Top) complete with
an imitation

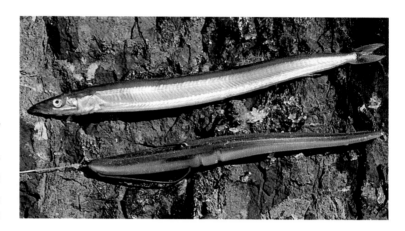

Latin name:	*Hyperoplus lanceolatus*
Description:	Very elongated fish with pointed head, silvery flanks and deep grey back – like the sandeels sold as bait but bigger!
Distribution:	Widespread throughout Cardigan Bay.
Preferred habitat:	A mid-water species, it is often caught in and around tidal rips and also from manmade structures by anglers feathering for mackerel.
Seasons:	Primarily a fish of the summer months.
Food:	A predator, it feeds on small fry swept along by the tide.
Eating:	Not generally eaten. Minimum size: 23cm (WFSA).
Welsh shore record:	Vacant as of January 2012.

Thick-lipped grey mullet

Photo: Rod Calbrade

Latin name:	*Chelon labrosus*
Description:	Grey backed, white-bellied with darker bands running lengthways along the flanks. The head appears small in proportion to the body and the mouth is likewise small, but the upper lip in particular is conspicuous in thickness, as opposed to the otherwise similar-looking thin-lipped grey mullet (*Liza ramada*).
Distribution:	Widespread around Cardigan Bay.
Preferred habitat:	This is an inshore and estuarine species that typically feeds over muddy substrates.
Seasons:	Spring to late autumn (depending on the weather).
Food:	Organic matter, tiny worms, protozoans, algae etc that it filters out from the mud that it consumes.
Eating:	Opinions differ widely. However, most mullet anglers regard them as a sportfishing species and release those they capture. Minimum size: 35cm.
Welsh shore record:	6.407kg/14lb 2oz (Aberthaw, South Wales, 1979). [Thin-lipped grey mullet – 1.191kg/2lb 10oz (Llangennech, Swansea, 1995).]

Golden-
grey mullet

Photo: Gareth Davies

Latin name:	*Liza aurata*
Description:	Similar to the other grey mullets except each gill-cover carries a conspicuous pale golden-yellow patch.
Distribution:	Localised populations in some inshore areas.
Preferred habitat:	Sandy surf beaches.
Seasons:	Summer.
Food:	Small crustaceans and worms.
Eating:	Good. Minimum size: 20cm (WFSA).
Welsh shore record:	1.333kg/2lb 15oz (Llangenith, Gower, 2007).

Red mullet

Photo: Carl & Pam Worrall

Latin name:	*Mullus surmuletus*
Description:	Distinctive, rather stocky fish with a blunt head sporting long barbels under the mouth. Red flanks, striped longitudinally; large scales.
Distribution:	Widespread but uncommon.
Preferred habitat:	Sandy or muddy seabeds seem to produce most catches.
Seasons:	Summer into autumn.
Food:	Crustaceans, worms, small shellfish, small fish.
Eating:	Highly-rated. Minimum size: 15cm (WFSA 18cm).
Welsh shore record:	840g/1lb 13.6oz (Cemlyn beach, Anglesey, 2008).

Sunfish

Photo: Gareth Davies

Latin name:	*Mola mola*
Description:	An often large and very distinctive-looking fish with a near-circular body profile when viewed from the side. Grey back, pale bluish-grey flanks and paler underside. Dorsal and anal fins are very long and it is sometimes spotted slowly swimming close to the surface with the dorsal protruding from the water, when it will often be accompanied above by a congregation of excited gulls.
Distribution:	Scattered as this is a species of the open oceans, but they can (and do) turn up pretty much anywhere in Cardigan Bay.
Preferred habitat:	Open oceans, drifting in part with the currents.
Seasons:	Sunfish tend to show during the warmer months of the year.
Food:	Jellyfish, small squid, crustaceans, fry, fish larvae and other planktonic organisms.
Eating:	Not regarded as an eating fish in the UK. They are uncommon, so if you do catch one, put it back.
Welsh shore record:	7.00kg/15lb 7oz (Point Lynas, Anglesey, 1995).

Angler fish
Photo: Gethyn Owen

Latin name:	*Lophius piscatorius*
Description:	Unmistakeable with a huge toothy mouth, broad head and large pectoral fins, the body tapering rapidly to a thinner tail.
Distribution:	Throughout Cardigan Bay, more frequent than angling catches would suggest as it is taken but rarely on rod and line.
Preferred habitat:	Over sand and mud, where it can lie in wait for passing prey.
Seasons:	All year round in deeper water.
Food:	Any passing fish that it can engulf: its stomach distends so that it can swallow prey close to its own size.
Eating:	The tail is sold commercially as 'Monkfish' (a source of confusion with the monkfish, *Squatina squatina*) and is good. Minimum size: 61cm (WFSA).
Welsh shore record:	29.03 kg/64lb (Mumbles, Swansea, 1985).

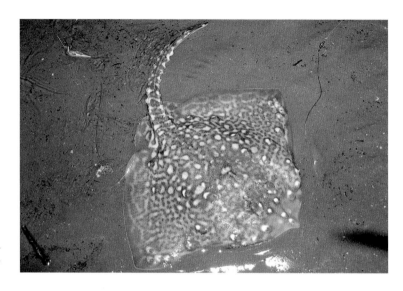

Thornback ray

Latin name:	*Raja clavata*
Description:	Typical ray shape with a mottled fawn and mid to deep brown back. There are a variable number of sharp, thornlike spines on the back and along the tail.
Distribution:	Widespread in Cardigan Bay but over-exploitation has severely reduced numbers.
Preferred habitat:	Over clean and sometimes mixed ground.
Seasons:	Spring–late autumn.
Food:	Fish and crustaceans primarily.
Eating:	Edible but catches of this slow-growing fish should always be returned to keep populations stable.
Welsh shore record:	8.2kg/18lb 1.25oz (Barry, South Wales, 2002).

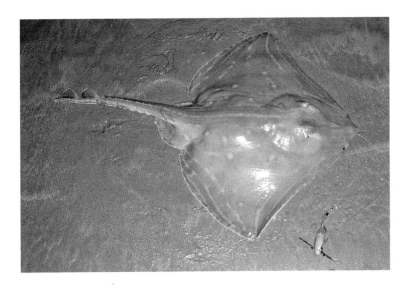

Small-eyed ray

Latin name:	*Raja microocellata*
Description:	Typical ray shape with sandy-coloured back marked by paler lines around the edges of the wings and blotches towards the middle.
Distribution:	Widespread in Cardigan Bay but populations tend to be localised to sandy areas.
Preferred habitat:	Clean, sandy ground.
Seasons:	Spring–late autumn.
Food:	Mostly fish, especially sand-eels.
Eating:	Edible but catches of this slow-growing fish should always be returned to keep populations stable.
Welsh shore record:	6.917kg/15lb 4oz (South Wales, 2008).

Spotted ray

Photo: Gareth Pickard

Latin name:	*Raja montagui*
Description:	A small ray with the typical shape; fairly evenly spotted in deep brown over a sandy background. Spots configured to form a vague circle on each wing.
Distribution:	Widespread but not abundant; an infrequent shore catch.
Preferred habitat:	Sandy patches adjacent to rocks with a preference for fairly deep water in general.
Seasons:	Late winter through spring into summer sees most catches.
Food:	Crustaceans and small fish.
Eating:	Edible but catches of this slow-growing fish should always be returned to keep populations stable.
Welsh shore record:	3.77kg/8lb 5oz (Mewslade, Gower, 1980).

Blonde ray

Photo: Gareth Davies

Latin name:	*Bathyraja brachyurops*
Description:	An often large ray, with even pattern of dark spots on a paler brown background.
Distribution:	Rare in Cardigan Bay: a possibility on clean ground from deepwater rock marks, but would be a very noteworthy catch. More frequently encountered 'round the corner', in the Bristol Channel.
Preferred habitat:	Clean ground with a reasonable depth of water.
Seasons:	Spring–late autumn.
Food:	Crustaceans, fish and molluscs.
Eating:	Edible but owing to its rarity any catches should be returned.
Welsh shore record:	13.636kg/30lb (Rhoscolyn, Anglesey, 1993).

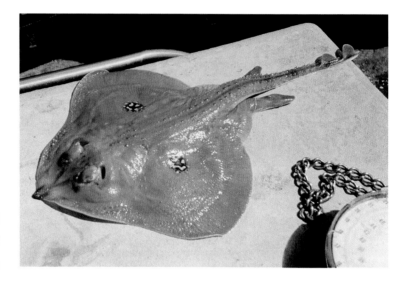

Cuckoo ray

Photo: Steve Hambidge

Latin name:	*Leucoraja naevus*
Description:	This is a straightforward ray to identify, being the only one in our waters with a single, large, black and yellow marbled spot in the middle of each otherwise unmarked pale brown wing. Small thorns run in rows down either side of the tail.
Distribution:	A fish of deeper water in general, although it does range through Cardigan Bay and is occasionally caught in shallow, inshore waters.
Preferred habitat:	Both clean and mixed ground have produced specimens.
Seasons:	Spring to late autumn.
Food:	A fairly varied diet that includes crustaceans, small fish and marine worms.
Eating:	Edible but rarity dictates that it should be returned.
Welsh shore record:	2.01kg/4lb 7oz (Porth Dafarch, Anglesey, 1981).

Stingray

Latin name:	*Dasyatis pastinaca*
Description:	A large, thickset ray with a smooth, brown to olive-brown slimy body and a thin, whip-like tail that carries the sting.
Distribution:	Widespread but not abundant; a very infrequent shore catch.
Preferred habitat:	Sandy shallows where it can bask in the sunshine.
Seasons:	Summer.
Food:	Crustaceans, worms and small fish.
Eating:	Not regarded as an eating fish.
Welsh shore record:	24.77kg/54lb 8oz (Fairbourne, Gwynedd, 1991).

Tope

Photo: Ian Pratt

Latin name:	*Galeorhinus galeus*
Description:	A medium to large shark, with a stereotypical long grey sharklike body and large mouth bristling with rows of sharp teeth.
Distribution:	Widespread in Cardigan Bay, especially but not exclusively offshore.
Preferred habitat:	Over both clean and rough ground depending on movements of prey fish.
Seasons:	Spring–autumn.
Food:	Other fish especially whiting, pouting, dabs and flounders.
Eating:	Not widely eaten as the flesh smells and tastes of ammonia. Minimum size: 140cm (WFSA).
Welsh shore record:	28.894kg/63lb 11oz (Trearddur Bay, Anglesey, 2008).

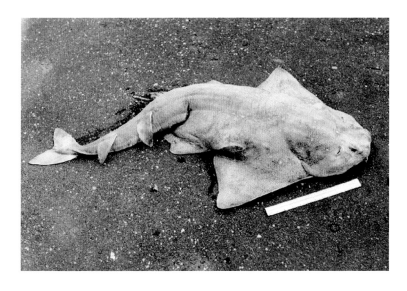

Monkfish
(also known as
angel shark)

Photo: Dr Jim Ellis, CEFAS

Latin name:	*Squatina squatina*
Description:	An often large fish with the peculiar appearance of being a mixture of a shark and a ray: elongate but with a flattened body with two sets of winglike fins, a sandy-coloured back for camouflage and a broad mouth equipped with sharp teeth.
Distribution:	Formerly found in scattered localities inshore around the bay, commercial pressure has rendered it extremely rare.
Preferred habitat:	Sand or mud, where it can bury itself in ambush.
Seasons:	Spring to late autumn.
Food:	Flatfish, other fish as available, crustaceans, molluscs.
Eating:	Any monkfish that are caught must be returned – they are protected by law.
Welsh shore record:	23.98kg/52lb 14oz (Llwyngwril, 1984).

Bull huss

(also known as
greater-spotted
dogfish)

Latin name:	*Scyliorhinus stellaris*
Description:	Large, powerfully-built dogfish; very rough brown skin with darker brown spots.
Distribution:	Throughout Cardigan Bay.
Preferred habitat:	Generally but not exclusively preferring deeper water, huss are also taken from shallow reefs and mixed ground beaches.
Seasons:	Late winter to late autumn sees the majority of catches, with spring a key time.
Food:	Huss will eat anything they can catch and swallow.
Eating:	Edible but hard work to skin: most anglers release them. Minimum size: 61cm (WFSA).
Welsh shore record:	9.015kg/19lb 14oz. (Pwllheli, 1992).

Lesser-spotted dogfish

Latin name:	*Scyliorhinus canicula*
Description:	The smallest of Cardigan Bay's sharks, an elongate light to dark brown fish with very rough skin and abundant mostly small spots. Dorsal fins begin behind the rear margins of the pelvic and anal fins: this helps distinguish them from small bull huss.
Distribution:	Widespread and very common in Cardigan Bay.
Preferred habitat:	Over all types of ground.
Seasons:	All year round, especially common inshore during spring and autumn.
Food:	Anything edible that it comes across.
Eating:	Edible once skinned. Minimum size: 45cm (WFSA).
Welsh shore record:	1.673kg/3lb 11oz (Fishguard, 2000).

Spurdog

Photo: Gethyn Owen

Latin name:	*Squalus acanthias*
Description:	A small to medium-sized grey shark, sometimes with a few white dots along the flanks. Both dorsal fins are preceded by very sharp spines, a unique feature in UK sharks.
Distribution:	Was widespread in Cardigan Bay but the population was decimated by long-lining: whether the stock will ever recover is a moot point, but it has reappeared off SW and NW Wales.
Preferred habitat:	Over many types of ground, often over sand and gravel.
Seasons:	Late autumn and early winter used to see occasional shore catches.
Food:	Spurdogs are active predators, feeding on any fish too slow to get out of the way.
Eating:	Good, but due to their fragile stocks catches should be returned. Minimum size: 61cm (WFSA).
Welsh shore record:	5.982kg/13lb 3oz (Anglesey, 1979).

Smooth-hound (starry)

Photo: Gareth Davies

Latin name:	*Mustelus mustelus* (common smoothound) and *Mustelus asterias* (starry smoothound)
Description:	Two similar-looking grey sharks; the starry has a variable pattern of pale dots on the back and flanks whilst the common is plain grey. Both have ray-like bony plates for crushing their food as opposed to the more usual shark-teeth.
Distribution:	Widespread around Cardigan Bay but populations tend to be localised.
Preferred habitat:	Clean to rough ground with a distinct preference for bouldery shores, where its prey tends to live.
Seasons:	Summer.
Food:	Crustaceans – primarily crabs and hermit-crabs.
Eating:	Edible but most anglers return them. Minimum size: 61cm (WFSA).
Welsh shore record:	8.282kg/18lb 4oz (common - Aberthaw, South Wales, 2011); 9.638kg/21lb 4oz (starry - Aberthaw, South Wales, 1998).

LAST CAST

I have included a few memorable fishing experiences in detail through these pages, but there are so many more from this past thirty years: the first time a cast went right (ah – so that's how it's done!); my first decent-sized bass, then my second just twenty minutes later; reeling in a dead weight one night, with a medium-sized ray emerging on the top hook of my rig and then gasping in amazement at the sight of a five-pound turbot that had taken the other bait (a double-shot I have never succeeded in repeating); fishing out there in a light surf on an August night in 2003, with the moon and Mars side-by-side, reflected clearly in the water tables; walking back along the clifftops near Aberdaron at sunset, the Wicklow Mountains low on the western horizon and Bardsey crystal-clear across the Sound, its myriad riptides still audible across the stillness. At such times, one is reminded that being there is what counts the most.

Then there were the times that things didn't go according to plan: the bad casts; tripping on the cobbles on the beach at Aberystwyth, bruising my knee cruelly and snapping my rod in two in the process; not understanding the conditions and driving fifty miles to a deep water rock mark only to find huge waves breaking over it; the blanks and the sessions in perfect conditions but where the weed made things impossible; wading out to cast and then getting back to my rod rest to find that someone's dog had eaten my bait; being the only angler on two miles of empty beach when a couple of surfers turned up and took to the waves just twenty metres away; the New Years' Eve when we vowed to stay out of the pub and instead fish an estuary mark and the mutual relief, about an hour later, when we decided to flee from the sub-zero easterly gale that was screaming by, whipping the sand up into clouds.

In these respects, shore angling is like any other activity: it has its great moments and its less than great moments, but the latter diminish in frequency over time as experience is gained and the advice in books and articles is tried, tested and the results absorbed and mentally filed away for later reference. Writing this has been like downloading a large part of my brain into my keyboard – over just a few weeks of intensive writing, the memories, like videos in my mind's eye have flowed out into words. Everything I have described or advised about in these pages has happened to me, and I hope that in time it happens to you – except for the broken rods and other mishaps. See you on the beach sometime ...

ABOUT THE AUTHOR

John Mason moved to Aberystwyth in 1981 to begin a degree in geology, and upon completing it he stayed in the area. Within months of arriving his interest in sea angling started and by the mid-1980s he was a regular at many shore fishing venues around Cardigan Bay and on the deep sea angling boats that sailed from Aberystwyth. Thirty years later his interest in catching his own supper is as strong as ever, and in early 2009 he set himself the challenge of catching forty species from the Welsh shore in a year, which he accomplished with a few weeks to spare early the following December. A writer and photographer too, he recorded the results of the species hunt with a view to providing a fish identification guide aimed at anglers, from which this book morphed into existence.